CW00341860

ORDER
MY STEPS
IN THY WORD
a study of Psalm 119

Delight Thyself
DESIGN MINISTRIES
delightthyself.com

Copyright © 2018 by Delight Thyself Design Ministries, Inc.

All Scripture quotations are taken from the King James Bible.

Published by Delight In Him Publications,
a division of Delight Thyself Design Ministries in Hurricane, WV.

Delight Thyself Design Ministries' mission is to design and distribute Gospel tracts for the furtherance of the Gospel of Jesus Christ. Our desire is to make tracts available to churches, while at the same time sending tracts to missionaries across the world in need of material.

All rights reserved. No part of this book may be reproduced or transmitted in any form or by any means - electronic, mechanical, photocopy, recording, or otherwise without written permission of the publisher, except for brief quotations in online or printed reviews.

Delight Thyself Design Ministries, Inc.
PO Box 725
Hurricane, WV 25526
delightthyself.com

Special thanks to those who gave their time as copy editors.

The contents of this book are the result of years of spiritual growth in life and ministry. Every effort has been made to give proper credit and attribution to quotes and information that is not original. It is not our intent to claim originality with any quote or thought that could not be tied to an original source.

Printed in the United States of America.

ISBN: 978-0-9995175-2-9

*To my parents
who taught me to love the Word of God.*

"ORDER MY STEPS IN THY WORD:
AND LET NOT ANY INIQUITY
HAVE DOMINION OVER ME."
PSALM 119:133

PSALM 119

Psalm 119 is the longest chapter in the Bible, which further explains just how much of a priority the Word of God should be in our lives.

The "Word of God Chapter of the Bible" includes 176 verses and gives us at least as many principles to live by. In nearly every verse there is at least one Word that refers to the Word of God.

Words referencing the Word of God:

Law of the Lord	Commandments
Testimonies	Judgments
Ways	Word
Precepts	Faithfulness
Statutes	Ordinances

When reading through the chapter, make an effort to find the specific Word within the verse that references the Word of God. Among the references are Truths about the Scripture that we can apply to our lives and allow It to encourage us in our walk with the Lord. **The Word of God magnifies Itself.** Later on in the Book of Psalms, the Scripture tells us that the Lord magnifies His Word even above His Name.

Psalm 138:2
*"I will worship toward thy holy temple, and praise thy name
for thy lovingkindness and for thy truth:
for thou hast magnified thy word above all thy name."*

Allow Psalm 119 to broaden your love for the Word.

Psalm 119:47
"And I will delight myself in thy commandments, which I have loved."

Delight in His Word today.

WALK IN HIS WORD.

Psalm 119:1
*"Blessed are the undefiled in the way,
who walk in the law of the LORD."*

WE ARE BLESSED WHEN WE WALK IN HIS WORD.
Psalm 1:1-3
"Blessed is the man that walketh not in the counsel of the ungodly, nor standeth in the way of sinners, nor sitteth in the seat of the scornful. But his delight is in the law of the LORD; and in his law doth he meditate day and night. And he shall be like a tree planted by the rivers of water, that bringeth forth his fruit in his season; his leaf also shall not wither; and whatsoever he doeth shall prosper."

Enoch lived 365 years, and he walked with God.
This shows us that we can walk with God every day of our lives.
We only need to set aside time to be with Him and delight in Him.

Psalm 112:1
"Praise ye the LORD. Blessed is the man that feareth the LORD, that delighteth greatly in his commandments."

Look into His Word today and every day.

James 1:25
"But whoso looketh into the perfect law of liberty, and continueth therein, he being not a forgetful hearer, but a doer of the work, this man shall be blessed in his deed."

IF WE WANT THE LORD
TO ORDER OUR STEPS,
WE MUST WALK IN HIS WORD.

Seek Him with Your Whole Heart.

Psalm 119:2
*"Blessed are they that keep his testimonies,
and that seek him with the whole heart."*

We are blessed when we obey His Word.
You can know all about the Bible, but if you do not obey
and apply it to your life, your knowledge is in vain.

Proverbs 2:1-6
*"My son, if thou wilt receive my words, and hide my commandments
with thee; So that thou incline thine ear unto wisdom, and apply thine
heart to understanding; Yea, if thou criest after knowledge,
and liftest up thy voice for understanding; If thou seekest her as silver,
and searchest for her as for hid treasures; Then shalt thou understand
the fear of the LORD, and find the knowledge of God.
For the LORD giveth wisdom: out of his mouth cometh
knowledge and understanding."*

We cannot understand until we first receive and hide His
commandments in our hearts, and we must also listen
and apply what we hear to our lives.

**We must seek and search for the Truth
before we will find the knowledge of God.**

Jeremiah 29:13
*"And ye shall seek me, and find me,
when ye shall search for me with all your heart."*

We have read the promise…if we seek Him, we will find Him.

**We must search for Him with our whole heart
and seek the Lord through His Word.**

**If we want the Lord
to order our steps,
we must seek Him
with our whole heart.**

AVOID THE SIN.

Psalm 119:3
"They also do no iniquity: they walk in his ways."

THOSE THAT SEEK THE LORD WALK IN HIS WORD INSTEAD OF WALKING IN SIN.
Our flesh craves sin and the pleasures of this world,
but the Word tells us that sin has consequences.

Psalm 66:18
"If I regard iniquity in my heart, the Lord will not hear me:"

What can we do to keep sin out of our heart? **We can avoid it.**

Proverbs 4:14-15
"Enter not into the path of the wicked, and go not in the way of evil men. Avoid it, pass not by it, turn from it, and pass away."

If we see sin around us, we must first stop and recognize it; then choose to turn around and go in a different direction. We can choose to avoid even the appearance of sin.
If it appears to be evil...it probably is.

1 Thessalonians 5:21-22
*"Prove all things; hold fast that which is good.
Abstain from all appearance of evil."*

When under attack, a soldier must have a plan in order to defeat the enemy. The armour of God consists mostly of defensive armour, but only one offensive weapon...The Sword of the Spirit. The Bible declares *"For the word of God is quick, and powerful, and sharper than any twoedged sword".*
We can avoid sin by hiding God's Word in our heart.

Psalm 119:11
"Thy word have I hid in mine heart, that I might not sin against thee."

 **IF WE WANT THE LORD TO ORDER OUR STEPS, WE MUST AVOID THE SIN IN OUR LIVES BY SPENDING TIME IN HIS WORD.**

DILIGENTLY READ.

Psalm 119:4
"Thou hast commanded us to keep thy precepts diligently."

WE MUST READ THE WORD OF GOD CAREFULLY, CONSISTENTLY AND CONSTANTLY.

To read just to be reading is not to read carefully.
To read just every now and then is not to read consistently.
To read just once a day is not to read constantly.

Deuteronomy 11:12-14
"A land which the Lord thy God careth for: the eyes of the Lord thy God are always upon it, from the beginning of the year even unto the end of the year. And it shall come to pass, if ye shall hearken diligently unto my commandments which I command you this day, to love the Lord your God, and to serve him with all your heart and with all your soul, That I will give you the rain of your land in his due season, the first rain and the latter rain, that thou mayest gather in thy corn, and thy wine, and thine oil."

If we are to diligently keep the Word in our hearts and minds, we must carefully, consistently, and constantly make the decision to do so.

**It takes faith to make the choice
to diligently seek Him through the Scripture.**

Hebrews 11:6
*"But without faith it is impossible to please him:
for he that cometh to God must believe that he is,
and that he is a rewarder of them that diligently seek him."*

 **IF WE WANT THE LORD
TO ORDER OUR STEPS,
WE MUST READ HIS WORD
DILIGENTLY & FAITHFULLY.**

DIRECTION.

Psalm 119:5
"O that my ways were directed to keep thy statutes!"

WE SHOULD NOT TAKE ONE STEP OF FAITH WITHOUT BEING DIRECTED BY THE WORD OF GOD.

In order for our ways to be directed, we must put our trust in the Lord and lean on His understanding instead of our own.

Proverbs 3:5-6
"Trust in the Lord with all thine heart;
and lean not unto thine own understanding.
In all thy ways acknowledge him, and he shall direct thy paths."

Our flesh desires to go in the complete opposite direction that God would have us to go.

This is why doing the right thing is sometimes one of the hardest things to do; but if we look into the Word, we will find the direction we need.

Proverbs 16:9
"A man's heart deviseth his way: but the Lord directeth his steps."

God desires to direct our steps through His Word.

He wants to guide us in the way we should go; if only we would take the time to read and meditate on what He has to say.

Psalm 32:8
"I will instruct thee and teach thee in the way which thou shalt go:
I will guide thee with mine eye."

IF WE WANT THE LORD TO ORDER OUR STEPS, WE MUST SEEK HIS DIRECTION THROUGH HIS WORD.

NOT ASHAMED.

Psalm 119:6
"Then shall I not be ashamed,
when I have respect unto all thy commandments."

WHEN OUR WAYS ARE DIRECTED BY OBEYING THE WORD OF GOD, WE WILL RESPECT THE SCRIPTURE AND THE TRUTH THAT IT CONTAINS..

When we have a right respect for God's Word,
we will not be ashamed of It.

"No shame in the presence of man will hinder us
when the fear of God has taken full possession of our minds."
C.H. Spurgeon

Romans 1:16
"For I am not ashamed of the gospel of Christ:
for it is the power of God unto salvation to every one that believeth;
to the Jew first, and also to the Greek."

Those who truly respect the Word of God
are not ashamed to proclaim It as Truth.

Since the Gospel of Jesus Christ is found within the Scripture, we can rightly apply that the Word "is the power of God unto salvation to every one that believeth." This power is available to anyone who chooses to believe that Jesus Christ died, was buried, and rose again to make a way for salvation for them.

We must desire to be grounded in the Scriptures so that we can develop a boldness to proclaim the Truth of the Gospel.

Psalm 119:80
"Let my heart be sound in thy statutes; that I be not ashamed."

IF WE WANT THE LORD
TO ORDER OUR STEPS,
WE MUST NOT BE ASHAMED
OF HIS WORD.

Uprightness of Heart.

Psalm 119:7
*"I will praise thee with uprightness of heart,
when I shall have learned thy righteous judgments."*

We cannot truly praise the Lord until we have learned from His Word..

We must have a teachable spirit within ourselves, listening to the Holy Spirit as He guides us through the Scripture. Along with being teachable, a prayerful attitude is necessary.

Psalm 25:4-5
*"Shew me thy ways, O LORD; teach me thy paths.
Lead me in thy truth, and teach me:
for thou art the God of my salvation; on thee do I wait all the day."*

As we prayerfully ask the Lord to teach and lead us, we will develop integrity, or uprightness of heart. We see this in the life of Solomon after he finished building the temple.

1 Kings 9:3-5
*"And the LORD said unto him, I have heard thy prayer and thy supplication, that thou hast made before me: I have hallowed this house, which thou hast built, to put my name there for ever; and mine eyes and mine heart shall be there perpetually. And if thou wilt walk before me, as David thy father walked, in integrity of heart, and in uprightness, to do according to all that I have commanded thee, and wilt keep my statutes and my judgments:
THEN I will establish the throne of thy kingdom upon Israel for ever, as I promised to David thy father, saying, There shall not fail thee a man upon the throne of Israel."*

God wanted to bless Solomon,
but He required some things of him beforehand;
and He requires the same thing of us...conditional blessings.

 **If we want the Lord to order our steps, we must learn His Word with uprightness of heart & praise Him accordingly.**

He Will Not Forsake Us.

Psalm 119:8
"I will keep thy statutes: O forsake me not utterly."

We See a Purpose Promised.
"I will keep thy statutes"
The Psalmist makes a promise that he will obey the Word of the Lord.

Have we promised to obey what He says?
Even when it's not easy?

We See a Prayerful Plea.
"O forsake me not utterly."
The Psalmist pleads with the Lord that He would not forsake him
or cast him away.

**We can rest assured today, because God has promised us
that will never leave us nor forsake us.**

Deuteronomy 31:6
*"Be strong and of a good courage, fear not, nor be afraid of them:
for the LORD thy God, he it is that doth go with thee;
he will not fail thee, nor forsake thee."*

We see this promise again in Hebrews
as a reminder that we should be content with what we have.

Hebrews 13:5
*"Let your conversation be without covetousness;
and be content with such things as ye have: for he hath said,
I will never leave thee, nor forsake thee. So that we may boldly say,
The Lord is my helper, and I will not fear what man shall do unto me."*

 **If we want the Lord
to order our steps,
we must obey His Word
remembering that
He will not forsake us.**

CLEANSED.

Psalm 119:9
*"Wherewithal shall a young man cleanse his way?
by taking heed thereto according to thy word."*

The first step in solving a problem is admitting there is a problem.
The Psalmist recognized that a cleansing was needed.

Do we even realize when there is sin in our lives?

WE CANNOT GET RID OF THE SIN THAT DISPLEASES THE LORD UNLESS WE FIRST ACKNOWLEDGE OUR SIN.

How can we cleanse our hearts?
By the Word of God.

If we want a cleansed heart, we must take heed to His Word.
Jesus spoke of being cleansed through the Words He speaks.

John 15:3
"Now ye are clean through the word which I have spoken unto you."

Desire a clean heart today, and prayerfully ask the Lord
to show you the sin that needs cleansed.

Psalm 51:10
*"Create in me a clean heart, O God;
and renew a right spirit within me.*

A cleansed heart is only a confession away.
No earthly priest is required. We can simply approach the throne of
grace to obtain mercy and find grace to help in time of need.

1 John 1:9
*"If we confess our sins, he is faithful and just to forgive us our sins,
and to cleanse us from all unrighteousness."*

 **IF WE WANT THE LORD TO ORDER OUR STEPS, WE MUST BE CLEANSED THROUGH HIS WORD.**

WANDERING.

Psalm 119:10
*"With my whole heart have I sought thee:
O let me not wander from thy commandments."*

ONCE WE SET OUT IN THE RIGHT DIRECTION, WE MUST REFUSE TO STRAY FROM THE PATH.

When we begin to compromise our beliefs, our behavior will start to change as well. Distractions will cause us to wander, and wandering is dangerous.

Proverbs 21:16
"The man that wandereth out of the way of understanding shall remain in the congregation of the dead."

The devil will use anything and anyone in order to distract us from God, His Word, and His purpose for our lives.

IT IS DANGEROUS TO LET OUR HEARTS & MINDS WANDER.

Our hearts are deceitful above all things, and our minds are wicked. We must keep ourselves focused upon the Lord through His Word to keep ourselves from wandering.

James 4:7
*"Submit yourselves therefore to God.
Resist the devil, and he will flee from you."*

If you are not distracted right now, you will be. God has given us the resources we need to keep our hearts and minds focused on Him.

Isaiah 26:3
*"Thou wilt keep him in perfect peace,
whose mind is stayed on thee: because he trusteth in thee."*

IF WE WANT THE LORD TO ORDER OUR STEPS, WE MUST KEEP OURSELVES FROM WANDERING FROM THE WORD.

Hidden Within Our Hearts.

Psalm 119:11
*"Thy word have I hid in mine heart,
that I might not sin against thee."*

If we hide God's Word within our hearts, we will be more prepared to resist the temptations of the devil.

The Psalmist does not desire to hide the Word in his mind, for knowledge will fail. He desires to hide God's Word within his heart. **Hiding the Word in your heart is to apply it to your life.**

"Thy word have I hid"
Nothing but the Word of God will keep us from sin.

"in mine heart"
We must apply the Word to our hearts for it to change our lives.

"that I might not sin"
We must purposefully decide in our hearts
to disregard the pleasures of sin.

"against thee."
When we sin, we are displeasing God.
We desire to please those we love; do we not desire to please God?

Only the Word of God can keep us from sin.

When Jesus was tempted by the devil, He did not use the words of man to resist him. He quoted Scripture. He showed us how we can defend ourselves against the wiles of the devil.

Matthew 4:10
*"Then saith Jesus unto him, Get thee hence, Satan: for it is written,
Thou shalt worship the Lord thy God, and him only shalt thou serve."*

If we want the Lord to order our steps, we must hide the Word of God in our hearts to keep us from sin.

A Teachable Heart.

Psalm 119:12
"Blessed art thou, O LORD: teach me thy statutes."

Do we desire to learn something from God's Word each time we read?

If our expectation is to not learn anything,
that will surely be our result.

We must be teachable, acknowledging that there is always something to learn from a passage or verse regardless of how well we think we already know It.

We cannot learn until we recognize that we have something to learn.

God desires us to ask Him to teach us.
Prayerfully ask the Lord to show you something
within His Word that you need for today.

Psalm 27:11
*"Teach me thy way, O LORD, and lead me in a plain path,
because of mine enemies."*

It is also important to make sure we are learning from the Right Source. There are many false teachers and preachers within our world today, many of whom teach from the wrong "bible". We are not helping, but rather hurting ourselves if we do not learn from the correct Word.

Psalm 86:11
*"Teach me thy way, O LORD; I will walk in thy truth:
unite my heart to fear thy name."*

 ## If we want the Lord to order our steps, we must open the Word with a teachable heart.

SPEAK.

Psalm 119:13
"With my lips have I declared all the judgments of thy mouth."

The Lord gave us lips to form the mouths from which we speak. How are we using our lips? What do we declare on a daily basis?

OUT OF THE LORD'S MOUTH IS THE VERY WORD OF GOD THAT WE HOLD IN OUR HANDS.

We are so unworthy of any part of Him, yet He chose to allow us to hold His Words with the hands He created.

It has been said many times before, "If you don't have anything nice to say, don't say anything at all." Those truthful words can be valuable to encourage us to maintain our testimony for the Lord. However, think of them in regard to God's Word.

IF WE DO NOT KNOW OR UNDERSTAND THE SCRIPTURE, THEN HOW CAN WE SPEAK ABOUT IT?

1 Peter 3:15-16
"But sanctify the Lord God in your hearts: and be ready always to give an answer to every man that asketh you a reason of the hope that is in you with meekness and fear: Having a good conscience; that, whereas they speak evil of you, as of evildoers, they may be ashamed that falsely accuse your good conversation in Christ."

We must read God's Word faithfully, and always be prepared to speak truthfully about what His Word says.

We cannot speak His Word if we have not first listened to Him.

 IF WE WANT THE LORD
TO ORDER OUR STEPS,
WE MUST REALIZE THAT IF WE ARE TO
SPEAK HIS WORD, WE MUST FIRST
LISTEN TO WHAT HE HAS TO SAY.

Rejoicing in the Way of the Word.

Psalm 119:14
"I have rejoiced in the way of thy testimonies, as much as in all riches."

Do we rejoice when we read the Bible?

The Psalmist considered the Scripture worth rejoicing over more than all the riches he could possess. He not only rejoiced in the Word but *"in the way of thy testimonies".*

John 14:6
"Jesus saith unto him, I am the way, the truth, and the life: no man cometh unto the Father, but by me."

As we read God's Word, we can praise the God of the Word and The Word Himself, Jesus Christ. His Word can bring us joy as we read the Scripture and are reminded that in His Word life can be found.

John 6:63
"It is the spirit that quickeneth; the flesh profiteth nothing: the words that I speak unto you, they are spirit, and they are life."

Jeremiah 15:16
"Thy words were found, and I did eat them; and thy word was unto me the joy and rejoicing of mine heart: for I am called by thy name, O LORD God of hosts."

As we seek Him through His Word, we will find rejoicing in our hearts.

Being reminded that we are called by His Name will surely put a smile on your face.

Psalm 40:16
"Let all those that seek thee rejoice and be glad in thee: let such as love thy salvation say continually, The LORD be magnified."

If we want the Lord to order our steps, we must take the time to rejoice in the Way of the Word.

MEDITATE UPON HIS WORD.

Psalm 119:15
"I will meditate in thy precepts, and have respect unto thy ways."

To meditate upon The Word is to contemplate, to ponder, and to pray as you read. We show our devotion to God and His Word when we take time to meditate upon what He has given us to read.

Psalm 1:2
"But his delight is in the law of the LORD;
and in his law doth he meditate day and night."

THE WORD OF GOD SHOULD CONSUME OUR THOUGHTS, AS WE ALLOW THE TRUTH TO BE APPLIED TO OUR LIVES.

We must have respect for the Holy Scriptures.
They are not just some man's words but the Words of the Almighty God. He preserved each Word so that we may have them today, and that alone should command our respect.

Spend time with the Lord today as you meditate upon His Word.

Joshua 1:8
"This book of the law shall not depart out of thy mouth;
but thou shalt meditate therein day and night,
that thou mayest observe to do according to all that is written
therein: for then thou shalt make thy way prosperous,
and then thou shalt have good success."

IF WE WANT THE LORD TO ORDER OUR STEPS, WE MUST TAKE THE TIME TO MEDITATE ON WHAT HIS WORD HAS TO SAY.

DELIGHT IN HIS WORD.

Psalm 119:16
"I will delight myself in thy statutes: I will not forget thy word."

We must make it a priority to delight in the Word of God.
Doing so will change our lives,
if only we will spend time in the Scriptures.

DELIGHTING IN HIS WORD WILL HELP US DEVELOP A LOVE FOR THE SCRIPTURES.

Psalm 119:47
"And I will delight myself in thy commandments, which I have loved."

DELIGHTING IN HIS WORD WILL MAKE US WANT TO FIND GOD'S WILL FOR OUR LIVES.

Psalm 40:8
"I delight to do thy will, O my God: yea, thy law is within my heart."

DELIGHTING IN HIS WORD CHANGES WHAT OUR HEARTS DESIRE.

God will give us the desires that line up with His will for our lives,
as we spend more time with Him.

Psalm 37:4
*"Delight thyself also in the LORD:
and he shall give thee the desires of thine heart."*

When we delight in His Word…
We can expect Him to direct us.
We can trust Him to provide for us.
We can have faith that He knows what is best for us.

IF WE WANT THE LORD TO ORDER OUR STEPS, WE MUST DELIGHT IN HIS WORD.

DEAL BOUNTIFULLY.

Psalm 119:17
"Deal bountifully with thy servant, that I may live, and keep thy word."

The Psalmist asks God to deal bountifully with him for a purpose. He asks for grace and mercy for a reason…so that he may live and obey God's Word.

When was the last time we begged God for His grace and mercy?

Psalm 119:124
*"Deal with thy servant according unto thy mercy,
and teach me thy statutes."*

If we do ask for His grace and mercy, what is our purpose in asking? If we ask for our own benefit or for our own desires, we are deceived.

WE HAVE THE OPPORTUNITY TO ASK FOR HIS GRACE AND MERCY BOLDLY AND WITH PURPOSE.

Hebrews 4:16
*"Let us therefore come boldly unto the throne of grace,
that we may obtain mercy, and find grace to help in time of need."*

**God bestows His grace and mercy upon us
as an undeserving people so that we may follow Him.**

 IF WE WANT THE LORD
TO ORDER OUR STEPS,
WE MUST ASK HIM
TO DEAL BOUNTIFULLY WITH US
THROUGH HIS WORD.

OPEN OUR EYES.

Psalm 119:18
*"Open thou mine eyes,
that I may behold wondrous things out of thy law."*

**Do we desire for the Lord to show us
something new each time we open our Bible?**

If we only read out of duty or obligation, we are reading in vain. We must desire God to speak to us through His Word while patiently listening to what He has to say.

IF WE WANT TO SEE WONDEROUS THINGS OUT OF THE WORD OF GOD, WE NEED ONLY ASK HIM TO SHOW US.

Jeremiah 33:3
*"Call unto me, and I will answer thee,
and show thee great and mighty things, which thou knowest not."*

There must be Light in order for us to see.
"Let there be light"
The first recorded Words spoken by God in Scripture.
God spoke, and there was Light.
In order for us to see, we must listen to what God has to say.

We have the Light of the World living inside of us to enlighten our hearts to the Truth of the Word. **The more we ask God to open our eyes by His Light, the more He will show us through His Word.**

Ephesians 1:17-18
"That the God of our Lord Jesus Christ, the Father of glory, may give unto you the spirit of wisdom and revelation in the knowledge of him: The eyes of your understanding being enlightened; that ye may know what is the hope of his calling, and what the riches of the glory of his inheritance in the saints,"

IF WE WANT THE LORD TO ORDER OUR STEPS, WE MUST BE WILLING TO HAVE OUR EYES OPENED TO THE TRUTH OF HIS WORD.

STRANGERS.

Psalm 119:19
"I am a stranger in the earth: hide not thy commandments from me."

The closer we are to God, the more uncomfortable we should feel in this world. People should look at us strangely and realize that there is something different about us. If they do not see a difference in us, then we are living like them. God calls us to not only be different, but to even be peculiar. There should be something distinguishable about God's children.

1 Peter 2:9-10
"But ye are a chosen generation, a royal priesthood, an holy nation, a peculiar people; that ye should shew forth the praises of him who hath called you out of darkness into his marvellous light; Which in time past were not a people, but are now the people of God: which had not obtained mercy, but now have obtained mercy."

How does the world view us? Do they think there is something strange about us? Do we stand out or do we blend in?

WE AS GOD'S PEOPLE ARE CALLED TO LET OUR LIGHT SHINE INTO THE DARKNESS OF THE WORLD.

Philippians 2:15-16
"That ye may be blameless and harmless, the sons of God, without rebuke, in the midst of a crooked and perverse nation, among whom ye shine as lights in the world; Holding forth the word of life; that I may rejoice in the day of Christ, that I have not run in vain, neither laboured in vain."

**May we shine our Light
by proclaiming the Word of Life in our daily lives!**
Those in darkness cannot see their sin
without the Light of the Gospel being shone on their hearts.

IF WE WANT THE LORD
TO ORDER OUR STEPS,
WE MUST LIVE AS STRANGERS
IN THIS WORLD.

LONGING FOR THE WORD.

Psalm 119:20
*"My soul breaketh for the longing
that it hath unto thy judgments at all times."*

DO WE LONG FOR OPENING UP THE WORD OF GOD AND DWELLING IN HIS PRESENCE?

"the longing"
An earnest desire to know and fully understand the Truth is pleasing to the Lord. The Psalmist desired this to the point that his soul was breaking.

Psalm 42:1-2
"As the hart panteth after the water brooks, so panteth my soul after thee, O God. My soul thirsteth for God, for the living God: when shall I come and appear before God?"

"at all times"
A constant craving for the Word will satisfy our souls.
May we long to read The Word of God, not just every now and then, but constantly and habitually with fervor and purpose.

A habit can only be formed when performed
over and over again in a consistent manner.
Our spiritual habits may well tell us the condition of our hearts.

Psalm 84:2
"My soul longeth, yea, even fainteth for the courts of the LORD: my heart and my flesh crieth out for the living God."

 IF WE WANT THE LORD
TO ORDER OUR STEPS,
WE MUST HAVE A LONGING FOR THE
WORD OF GOD.

REPLACE THE PRIDE.

Psalm 119:21
"Thou hast rebuked the proud that are cursed, which do err from thy commandments."

A proud person magnifies himself above those around him.
One of the six things which the Lord hates is a proud look. When we have pride within our hearts, we cannot please the Lord.

James 4:6
"But he giveth more grace. Wherefore he saith, God resisteth the proud, but giveth grace unto the humble."

PRIDE WILL KEEP US FROM THE WORD OF GOD.
Likewise, keeping ourselves away from the Word will develop pride in our hearts. We must remove anything within our lives that causes us to do anything contrary to what the Scriptures tell us.

Proverbs 19:27
"Cease, my son, to hear the instruction that causeth to err from the words of knowledge."

Acknowledging pride within ourselves should persuade us to cling more closely to the Scriptures.

Luke 11:28
*"But he said, Yea rather,
blessed are they that hear the word of God, and keep it."*

 IF WE WANT THE LORD
TO ORDER OUR STEPS,
WE MUST REPLACE THE PRIDE
WITHIN OUR HEARTS
WITH THE WORD OF GOD.

WEIGHED DOWN.

Psalm 119:22
"Remove from me reproach and contempt;
for I have kept thy testimonies."

When we are weighed down by the actions of others, the Word of God can soothe our hurting souls and advise what is best for us.

The Psalmist asked for reproach and contempt to be removed from him, or rolled off of his shoulders. He desired that the burden be transferred to Someone else.

Psalm 37:5
"Commit thy way unto the LORD; trust also in him;
and he shall bring it to pass."

God wants us to commit our burdens to Him by rolling them off of our shoulders and allowing Him to carry them. He sometimes uses willing Christians to help bear the burdens of others. He may even want to use us to help someone else, if only we are willing to do so.

Galatians 6:2
"Bear ye one another's burdens, and so fulfil the law of Christ."

WHAT IS WEIGHING YOU DOWN TODAY?
Give it to the Lord and allow Him to carry it.

Do you know of someone hurting today?
Help them bear their burden.
Someday they may need to help you carry yours.

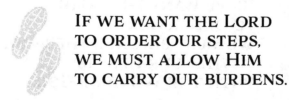

IF WE WANT THE LORD
TO ORDER OUR STEPS,
WE MUST ALLOW HIM
TO CARRY OUR BURDENS.

Encouraged By The Word.

Psalm 119:23
"Princes also did sit and speak against me:
but thy servant did meditate in thy statutes."

No matter who chooses to speak against or about us,
we can choose to focus on what God has to say in His Word.
Despite what was being said about him, the Psalmist did not let it distract him from seeking help from the Lord.

1 Samuel 30:6
"And David was greatly distressed; for the people spake of stoning him, because the soul of all the people was grieved, every man for his sons and for his daughters: but David encouraged himself in the LORD his God."

We can choose to follow David's example,
for it was in times when he was discouraged and distressed that he sought encouragement from the Lord.

He knew that within the Word of God was the answer to his problem.

How do you encourage yourself in times of distress?
What is your first resource for help?

Hebrews 4:12
"For the word of God is quick, and powerful, and sharper than any twoedged sword, piercing even to the dividing asunder of soul and spirit, and of the joints and marrow, and is a discerner of the thoughts and intents of the heart."

If we want the Lord to order our steps, we must seek to be encouraged by the Word of God.

COMFORT & COUNSEL.

Psalm 119:24
"Thy testimonies also are my delight and my counselors."

In just these nine words, we find so much Truth about the Blessed Book we hold in our hands. We see here two purposes in this Scripture that we must apply to our lives.

THE WORD OF GOD CAN COMFORT US.
"Thy testimonies also are my delight"
In the darkness of night or the dreariness of the day, we can be comforted if we will open our Bible. **It is wonderful to know that comfort can be found in times of distress.**

Psalm 94:19
*"In the multitude of my thoughts within me
thy comforts delight my soul."*

The world offers only temporary relief from our problems.
Comfort brings peace; but true peace only comes from God.

Philippians 4:7
*"And the peace of God, which passeth all understanding,
shall keep your hearts and minds through Christ Jesus.*

THE WORD OF GOD CAN COUNSEL US.
"Thy testimonies also are…my counselors."
The Bible offers us instruction and correction. Sometimes we need to be told we are wrong, and it is up to us to take heed to the Truth. We can choose to ignore the instruction, or apply the correction to our hearts and allow God to use our lives for His glory.

Colossians 3:16
"Let the word of Christ dwell in you richly in all wisdom; teaching and admonishing one another in psalms and hymns and spiritual songs, singing with grace in your hearts to the Lord."

IF WE WANT THE LORD
TO ORDER OUR STEPS,
WE MUST SEEK BOTH COMFORT AND
COUNSEL FROM THE WORD OF GOD.

QUICKENED BY THE WORD.

Psalm 119:25
*"My soul cleaveth unto the dust:
quicken thou me according to thy word."*

WHEN PROBLEMS ARE ALL AROUND US, IT CAN AFFECT US PHYSICALLY, EMOTIONALLY, AND EVEN SPIRITUALLY.

Here we see that the Psalmist is cleaving unto the dust. In Genesis we learn that we were made from the dust of the earth, so he is clinging to return to the dust in death.

Thankfully, he did not stop at his desire to end all of his problems. He sought a Solution.

"quicken thou me according to thy word"
The word *"quicken"* means to be made alive.
Rather than cleave to the dust where he came from, the Psalmist chose to be made alive by the Scriptures.
He knew there was resurrecting power within the Word of God!

John 6:63
"It is the spirit that quickeneth; the flesh profiteth nothing: the words that I speak unto you, they are spirit, and they are life."

There is power in His Word, and it is available to us, if only we would read and apply it to our lives.

Psalm 143:11
*"Quicken me, O LORD, for thy name's sake:
for thy righteousness' sake bring my soul out of trouble."*

IF WE WANT THE LORD TO ORDER OUR STEPS, WE MUST DESIRE TO BE QUICKENED BY THE WORD OF GOD.

Declare Our Ways.

Psalm 119:26
*"I have declared my ways, and thou heardest me:
teach me thy statutes."*

When We Confess Our Sins,
The Lord Not Only Hears Us,
He Forgives Us.

Psalm 32:5
*"I acknowledged my sin unto thee, and mine iniquity have I not hid.
I said, I will confess my transgressions unto the LORD;
and thou forgavest the iniquity of my sin. Selah."*

If we do not confess our sins, the Lord will not hear our prayers.

Psalm 66:18
"If I regard iniquity in my heart, the Lord will not hear me:"

After David confessed his sin and acknowledged his faith
that the Lord heard him, he desired to be taught
by the Teacher of all teachers.

What is standing in the way of the Lord hearing our prayers?
Are we willing to allow the Lord to teach us through His Word?

Psalm 86:11
*"Teach me thy way, O LORD; I will walk in thy truth:
unite my heart to fear thy name."*

The phrase *"teach me"* appears nine times within Psalm 119.

If We Want the Lord
To Order Our Steps,
We Must Declare Our Ways
And Ask the Lord to Teach Us
Through His Word.

UNDERSTAND THE WAY.

Psalm 119:27
*"Make me to understand the way of thy precepts:
so shall I talk of thy wondrous works."*

MAY WE DESIRE TO UNDERSTAND MORE AND MORE THE SCRIPTURES WE READ EACH DAY.

Seek to know, apply, and walk within the Way of the Word of God.

Hosea 14:9
"Who is wise, and he shall understand these things? prudent, and he shall know them? for the ways of the Lord are right, and the just shall walk in them: but the transgressors shall fall therein."

To understand the way of the Scriptures is to discern them by way of the Holy Spirit speaking to our hearts as we read.

John 16:13
"Howbeit when he, the Spirit of truth, is come, he will guide you into all truth: for he shall not speak of himself; but whatsoever he shall hear, that shall he speak: and he will shew you things to come."

1 Corinthians 2:13-14
"Which things also we speak, not in the words which man's wisdom teacheth, but which the Holy Ghost teacheth; comparing spiritual things with spiritual. But the natural man receiveth not the things of the Spirit of God: for they are foolishness unto him: neither can he know them, because they are spiritually discerned."

As we begin to understand the way, we can share the wonderful things we learn and experience as we fellowship with the Lord.
It is by God's grace that we may know of His wondrous works.

Psalm 111:4
*"He hath made his wonderful works to be remembered:
the LORD is gracious and full of compassion."*

IF WE WANT THE LORD TO ORDER OUR STEPS, WE MUST SEEK TO UNDERSTAND THE WAY HE WOULD HAVE US TO GO.

STRENGTHENED BY THE WORD.

Psalm 119:28
*"My soul melteth for heaviness:
strengthen thou me according unto thy word."*

**When circumstances cause our hearts to be heavy within us,
the Solution can be found within the pages of the Scriptures.**

Matthew 11:28
*"Come unto me, all ye that labour and are heavy laden,
and I will give you rest."*

Our Saviour is patiently waiting while bidding us to come to Him. Though the problem may not immediately disappear, He can speak peace to the storms within our heart through His Word. There is a verse for every situation and enough strength for every weakness.

Psalm 27:14
*"Wait on the LORD: be of good courage,
and he shall strengthen thine heart: wait, I say, on the LORD."*

Psalm 73:26
*"My flesh and my heart faileth: but God is the strength of my heart,
and my portion for ever."*

Isaiah 40:28-29
"Hast thou not known? hast thou not heard, that the everlasting God, the LORD, the Creator of the ends of the earth, fainteth not, neither is weary? there is no searching of his understanding. He giveth power to the faint; and to them that have no might he increaseth strength."

**THOUGH OUR STRENGTH MAY FAIL US, WE CAN CHOOSE
TO DO EVERYTHING THROUGH HIS STRENGTH.**

Philippians 4:13
"I can do all things through Christ which strengtheneth me."

**IF WE WANT THE LORD
TO ORDER OUR STEPS,
WE MUST SEEK TO BE STRENGTHENED
BY THE WORD OF GOD.**

Discern The Difference.

Psalm 119:29
"Remove from me the way of lying: and grant me thy law graciously."

David desired for the sin of lying to be removed from his life.
He was concerned with being delivered from more than just lying,
but from the falsehood and deception of other beliefs and doctrines.
He desired for the Truth of God's Word to be applied to his life.

Psalm 119:104
*"Through thy precepts I get understanding:
therefore I hate every false way."*

There is so much deception in religion today that we must be able to
discern what is right or wrong.

How are we to discern the difference?

James 1:5
*"If any of you lack wisdom, let him ask of God, that giveth to all men
liberally, and upbraideth not; and it shall be given him."*

Proverbs 2:6-7
*"For the LORD giveth wisdom: out of his mouth cometh knowledge
and understanding. He layeth up sound wisdom for the righteous: he
is a buckler to them that walk uprightly."*

We need only ask, and the Lord will give it to us.
Wisdom and discernment are found within the pages
of Scripture, the very Words of God.

Notice how David asks to receive the Law…*"graciously".*

Within the Word of God is the Gospel given by His grace.
For it is by His grace we are saved
through faith in His finished work.

If we want the Lord to order our steps, we must discern the difference between right and wrong by His grace.

MAKE THE CHOICE.

Psalm 119:30
"I have chosen the way of truth: thy judgments have I laid before me."

When Jesus spoke to Mary and Martha, showing them the difference in their priorities, He also left us an example to follow.

Luke 10:41-42
*"And Jesus answered and said unto her, Martha, Martha,
thou art careful and troubled about many things:
But one thing is needful: and Mary hath chosen that good part,
which shall not be taken away from her."*

But what was *"that good part"* that Mary chose?

Luke 10:39
*"And she had a sister called Mary, which also sat at Jesus' feet,
and heard his word."*

MARY MADE THE CHOICE.
She chose to sit at the feet of her Saviour
and listen to what He had to say.

**We must make the choice to learn from,
listen to, and love the Word of God.**

We must also make the choice to follow the *"way of truth"* rather than false doctrine. When we feel overwhelmed or need help to continue in the Word, we can simply ask the Lord to help us.

Psalm 119:173
"Let thine hand help me; for I have chosen thy precepts."

IF WE WANT THE LORD
TO ORDER OUR STEPS,
WE MUST MAKE THE CHOICE
TO APPLY GOD'S WORD TO OUR LIVES.

Adhere To The Word.

Psalm 119:31
"I have stuck unto thy testimonies: O LORD, put me not to shame."

After we make the choice to apply God's Word, we must then consistently choose to adhere to His Word.

In order to follow through with our choice, we must make our walk with Him consistent and constant. David wanted to stick with the right way and not be found unfaithful.

Psalm 63:7-8
"Because thou hast been my help, therefore in the shadow of thy wings will I rejoice. My soul followeth hard after thee: thy right hand upholdeth me."

Who is seated at the right hand of the Father? David knew the importance of Jesus Christ upholding him each day as he walked with God.

John 8:31-32
"Then said Jesus to those Jews which believed on him, If ye continue in my word, then are ye my disciples indeed; And ye shall know the truth, and the truth shall make you free."

We must cling to the Word each day.
Do you desire to read the Scriptures, or are you reading out of obligation?

Job 23:11-12
"My foot hath held his steps, his way have I kept, and not declined. Neither have I gone back from the commandment of his lips; I have esteemed the words of his mouth more than my necessary food."

We must crave the Word each day.
For our spirit needs nourishment as often, if not more often than our physical body.

If we want the Lord to order our steps, we must choose to adhere to the Word of God consistently.

RUN.

Psalm 119:32
*"I will run the way of thy commandments,
when thou shalt enlarge my heart."*

We are familiar with the need to walk with the Lord, but have we ever run with Him? Running implies that there is swiftness and a delight in our pace when journeying with Him.

1 Corinthians 9:24
"Know ye not that they which run in a race run all, but one receiveth the prize? So run, that ye may obtain. And every man that striveth for the mastery is temperate in all things. Now they do it to obtain a corruptible crown; but we an incorruptible. I therefore so run, not as uncertainly; so fight I, not as one that beateth the air:"

We need not run in vain or amiss, but rather with a goal in mind.

Hebrews 12:1
"Wherefore seeing we also are compassed about with so great a cloud of witnesses, let us lay aside every weight, and the sin which doth so easily beset us, and let us run with patience the race that is set before us,"

THE SCRIPTURE TELLS US THE DIRECTION WE NEED TO RUN TOWARD.

Hebrews 12:2
"Looking unto Jesus the author and finisher of our faith; who for the joy that was set before him endured the cross, despising the shame, and is set down at the right hand of the throne of God."

**The Lord is willing to enlarge our hearts
with more knowledge and wisdom through His Word.**
As we love Him more, our hearts will grow.

IF WE WANT THE LORD
TO ORDER OUR STEPS,
WE MUST BE WILLING TO RUN
TO HIM THROUGH HIS WORD.

Ask Him To Teach Us.

Psalm 119:33
*"Teach me, O LORD, the way of thy statutes;
and I shall keep it unto the end."*

There is no better teacher
of the Scripture than the Lord.
There is no telling what we could learn if we would simply
ask Him to teach us before we even read a Word.

Job 36:22
"Behold, God exalteth by his power: who teacheth like him?"

As David prays for the Lord to teach His Word to him, he makes a
commitment to show his sincerity. *"I shall keep it unto the end."* He
vows that if God would teach him the Way of the Word, he would
obey the Word the rest of his days. He desired the manner of his life
mirror what God's Word said.

Should we not want the same for our lives?
**Oh the benefits that are available to us
if only we would obey the Scripture!**

Proverbs 3:1-2
*"My son, forget not my law; but let thine heart
keep my commandments: For length of days, and long life,
and peace, shall they add to thee."*

We can only obey the Word if we have first been
taught what the Word says.
When was the last time you asked Him to teach you?

Psalm 143:10
*"Teach me to do thy will; for thou art my God: thy spirit is good;
lead me into the land of uprightness."*

 **If we want the Lord
to order our steps,
we must ask Him to teach us
so that we can obey.**

GIVE ME UNDERSTANDING.

Psalm 119:34
*"Give me understanding, and I shall keep thy law;
yea, I shall observe it with my whole heart."*

Five times throughout this chapter on the Word of God,
David sincerely requests, *"Give me understanding".*

AN UNDERSTANDING TO OBEY.
Psalm 119:34
*"Give me understanding, and I shall keep thy law;
yea, I shall observe it with my whole heart."*

AN UNDERSTANDING TO LEARN.
Psalm 119:73
*"Thy hands have made me and fashioned me:
give me understanding, that I may learn thy commandments."*

AN UNDERSTANDING TO SERVE.
Psalm 119:125
*"I am thy servant; give me understanding,
that I may know thy testimonies."*

AN UNDERSTANDING TO LIVE RIGHTEOUSLY.
Psalm 119:144
*"The righteousness of thy testimonies is everlasting:
give me understanding, and I shall live."*

AN UNDERSTANDING TO PRAY.
Psalm 119:169
*"Let my cry come near before thee, O LORD:
give me understanding according to thy word."*

What type of understanding do you need today?
God's Word has the answer to any problem that you face.

**IF WE WANT THE LORD
TO ORDER OUR STEPS,
WE MUST BE WILLING TO ASK
FOR UNDERSTANDING.**

In The Path.

Psalm 119:35
*"Make me to go in the path of thy commandments;
for therein do I delight."*

In order to walk in this path, we must open God's Word and allow His Words to light the way.

Psalm 119:105
"Thy word is a lamp unto my feet, and a light unto my path."

**As the Light brightens our hearts, His presence fills us with joy
as He begins to reveal the path for our lives.**

Psalm 16:11
*"Thou wilt shew me the path of life: in thy presence is fulness of joy;
at thy right hand there are pleasures for evermore."*

When our hearts feel weary,
He restores us through His Word and leads us for His glory.

Psalm 23:3
*"He restoreth my soul: he leadeth me
in the paths of righteousness for his name's sake."*

We must trust in the Lord and acknowledge Him
so that He can direct our paths as He sees fit.

Proverbs 3:6
"In all thy ways acknowledge him, and he shall direct thy paths."

 **If we want the Lord
to order our steps,
we must live in the path
of His Word.**

DESIRE THE WORD.

Psalm 119:36
"Incline my heart unto thy testimonies, and not to covetousness."

IT IS NOT A NATURAL THING FOR OUR HEARTS TO CRAVE THE WORD OF GOD.
Even as born again believers,
we are still wrapped in the flesh and our hearts are still wicked.

Jeremiah 17:9
*"The heart is deceitful above all things,
and desperately wicked: who can know it?"*

Our hearts are wicked,
but because Christ lives in us we are new creatures through Him.
He can give us the desire to want to know more through His Word.

Proverbs 2:2
*"So that thou incline thine ear unto wisdom,
and apply thine heart to understanding;"*

**We can choose to apply our hearts to the Word of God
and develop a yearning for the Truth.**

ASK THE LORD TO GIVE YOU A DESIRE FOR THE WORD.

1 Peter 2:2-3
*"As newborn babes, desire the sincere milk of the word, that ye may
grow thereby: If so be ye have tasted that the Lord is gracious."*

 **IF WE WANT THE LORD
TO ORDER OUR STEPS,
WE MUST DESIRE
THE WORD OF GOD.**

ALL IS VANITY.

Psalm 119:37
*"Turn away mine eyes from beholding vanity;
and quicken thou me in thy way."*

WE MUST CHOOSE TO LOOK AWAY
WHEN CONFRONTED WITH SIN.

In the world that we live in today, there is vanity all around us.

WHAT WE SEE WITH OUR EYES
AFFECTS THE CONDITION OF OUR HEART.

In the Book of Ecclesiastes we see chapter after chapter of the regret of Solomon having chosen the vain things of this world.

Ecclesiastes 1:14
*"I have seen all the works that are done under the sun;
and, behold, all is vanity and vexation of spirit."*

**Rather than living in vanity,
we must choose to allow the Word of God to strengthen us
to continue walking with and for the Lord Jesus Christ.**

Romans 12:1-2
*"I beseech you therefore, brethren, by the mercies of God,
that ye present your bodies a living sacrifice, holy, acceptable unto
God, which is your reasonable service. And be not conformed to this
world: but be ye transformed by the renewing of your mind,
that ye may prove what is that good, and acceptable,
and perfect, will of God."*

Philippians 3:13-14
*"Brethren, I count not myself to have apprehended: but this one thing
I do, forgetting those things which are behind, and reaching forth
unto those things which are before, I press toward the mark for the
prize of the high calling of God in Christ Jesus."*

IF WE WANT THE LORD
TO ORDER OUR STEPS,
WE MUST LOOK AWAY FROM VANITY,
AND ALLOW THE WORD TO BE OUR
GUIDE.

Establish The Word.

Psalm 119:38
"Stablish thy word unto thy servant, who is devoted to thy fear."

Rather than plead for himself to be established,
he asks for the Word of God to be established within him.

This is something that every Christian should desire.
Rather than the world seeing us, may it see Him.
Rather than others remembering what we say, may they only
remember the Word of God that we spoke to them.
David desired this and so did Paul; but do we?

As we have the Word of God established within us, may we stand so that others may see Him.

1 Corinthians 2:1-5
*"And I, brethren, when I came to you, came not with excellency of
speech or of wisdom, declaring unto you the testimony of God.
For I determined not to know any thing among you, save Jesus Christ,
and him crucified. And I was with you in weakness, and in fear,
and in much trembling. And my speech and my preaching was not
with enticing words of man's wisdom, but in demonstration of the
Spirit and of power: That your faith should not stand in the wisdom of
men, but in the power of God."*

We must not seek the wisdom of men but the wisdom that God has available to us.

This wisdom begins with seeking God through His Word
and coming to the Scriptures with a godly fear.
To fear the Lord is to have reverence for Him
and each Word that He has preserved for us.

Proverbs 9:10
*"The fear of the LORD is the beginning of wisdom:
and the knowledge of the holy is understanding."*

If we want the Lord to order our steps, we must ask Him to establish His Word in our hearts.

FEAR THE REPROACHES.

Psalm 119:39
"Turn away my reproach which I fear: for thy judgments are good."

The Psalmist feared that he would get in the way or interfere with the Lord's work. Oh, that we all had this attitude! **We should never lose the fear of hindering something He desires to do by depending on ourselves.**

THE REPROACH OF SIN.

Psalm 39:8
*"Deliver me from all my transgressions:
make me not the reproach of the foolish."*

David feared that his sin would hinder someone else from having faith in the Lord. Our individual sin could deter someone from seeing the Truth, but our nation's sin could distract others as well.

Proverbs 14:34
*"Righteousness exalteth a nation:
but sin is a reproach to any people."*

THE REPROACH OF SCORN.

Sometimes we do not even realize the result of scorn within our lives. **Our words and our opinions can occasionally do more harm than good.**

Psalm 79:4
*"We are become a reproach to our neighbours,
a scorn and derision to them that are round about us."*

"for thy judgments are good."
Though reproach can have its effects, the Word of the Lord will never return void. May we remember to yield to the Holy Spirit working in and through us, instead of becoming a hindrance; **for it is not us that can do the work but Christ in us that can make the difference.**

IF WE WANT THE LORD
TO ORDER OUR STEPS,
WE MUST FEAR HINDERING OTHERS
IN THEIR WALK WITH THE LORD.

Evaluate.

Psalm 119:40
*"Behold, I have longed after thy precepts:
quicken me in thy righteousness."*

Avoiding or Adoring?
Complaining or Craving?
Dreading or Desiring?
Leaving or Longing?

WE CAN CHOOSE OUR ATTITUDE
IS WHEN APPROACHING THE WORD OF GOD.

Psalm 119:9-12
"Wherewithal shall a young man cleanse his way? by taking heed thereto according to thy word. With my whole heart have I sought thee: O let me not wander from thy commandments. Thy word have I hid in mine heart, that I might not sin against thee. Blessed art thou, O LORD: teach me thy statutes."

Those days we just do not feel like reading or studying the Word are the ones we need It the most. Yet far too often we allow our flesh to get the best of us, as we make excuses or promises to do better or even more tomorrow.

IT IS TIME FOR US TO EVALUATE OUR MOTIVES
AND OUR ATTITUDES CONCERNING THE WORD OF GOD.

"quicken me in thy righteousness."
**Do we desire to be made more alive
by the Words of our Almighty God?**

IF WE WANT THE LORD
TO ORDER OUR STEPS,
WE MUST EVALUATE OURSELVES
CONCERNING THE WORD OF GOD.

Thankful For God's Mercy.

Psalm 119:41
*"Let thy mercies come also unto me, O LORD,
even thy salvation, according to thy word."*

Mercy involves not getting what we actually deserve.
God spares us because of His love for us, and through His grace,
He bestows upon us more than we could ever deserve or merit.

Where would we be without God's mercy?
There are times when we need to ask God to have mercy on us, and
there are other times when He gives it to us without our knowledge.

God's Mercy In Salvation.
We could not and cannot earn our salvation. Nothing we could ever
do on our own would merit eternal life in Heaven, but God provided
us the Way. We need only accept the free gift of salvation through
Jesus Christ our Lord and Saviour by God's mercy and grace!

Titus 3:4-7
*"But after that the kindness and love of God our Saviour toward man
appeared, Not by works of righteousness which we have done, but
according to his mercy he saved us, by the washing of regeneration,
and renewing of the Holy Ghost; Which he shed on us abundantly
through Jesus Christ our Saviour; That being justified by his grace, we
should be made heirs according to the hope of eternal life."*

God's Mercy In Deliverance.
He is Faithful to hear us when we call upon Him. In times of trouble, it
is His mercy upon which we can rely. He is Merciful to deliver us from
times of distress, even those we bring upon ourselves. Our failures
can disappear, because He never fails.

Psalm 4:1
*"Hear me when I call, O God of my righteousness: thou hast enlarged
me when I was in distress; have mercy upon me, and hear my prayer."*

 **If we want the Lord
to order our steps,
we must be thankful
for His mercy.**

Merciful While Trusting.

Psalm 119:42
*"So shall I have wherewith to answer him that reproacheth me:
for I trust in thy word."*

When we find ourselves hurting due to someone's doing or lack of responsibility, our flesh's first instinct is to get even.

A reproach against us is not a license to get vengeance.

Instead, we have the option of offering
a prayerful request to have mercy on others.

IF WE WANT TO RECEIVE MERCY WHEN WE NEED IT, WE OURSELVES MUST FIRST BE MERCIFUL.

Matthew 5:7
"Blessed are the merciful: for they shall obtain mercy."

During the first part of the Sermon on the Mount, the Lord Jesus Christ gave nine descriptions of Blessed people. It is no coincidence that He spoke about mercy in the fifth verse, five being the number of grace. God's mercy is always accompanied by His grace.

"for I trust in thy word."
May we be merciful while trusting in the Truth of the Word of God.

Psalm 56:4
*"In God I will praise his word, in God I have put my trust;
I will not fear what flesh can do unto me."*

Psalm 56:10-11
"In God will I praise his word: in the LORD will I praise his word. In God have I put my trust: I will not be afraid what man can do unto me."

IF WE WANT THE LORD TO ORDER OUR STEPS, WE MUST BE MERCIFUL WHILE TRUSTING IN THE WORD OF GOD.

THE WORD OF TRUTH.

Psalm 119:43
"And take not the word of truth utterly out of my mouth;
or I have hoped in thy judgments."

JESUS CHRIST IS THE WORD.
John 1:1,14
"In the beginning was the Word, and the Word was with God, and
the Word was God. And the Word was made flesh, and dwelt among
us, (and we beheld his glory, the glory as of the only begotten of the
Father,) full of grace and truth."

JESUS CHRIST IS THE TRUTH.
John 14:6
"Jesus saith unto him, I am the way, the truth, and the life:
no man cometh unto the Father, but by me."

So in studying the Word of Truth,
we can find Christ within every page.

He is there, within the pages of the Scripture that He has preserved
for us. He is there, within the Word where we read of the Gospel that
He provided for us.

1 Peter 1:24-25
"For all flesh is as grass, and all the glory of man as the flower of grass.
The grass withereth, and the flower thereof falleth away:
But the word of the Lord endureth for ever.
And this is the word which by the gospel is preached unto you."

"And take not the word of truth utterly out of my mouth"
We have been given the Word of Truth so that we may read and
study the Scriptures so that we can speak truthfully.

2 Timothy 2:15
"Study to shew thyself approved unto God, a workman that needeth
not to be ashamed, rightly dividing the word of truth."

IF WE WANT THE LORD
TO ORDER OUR STEPS,
WE MUST SEEK TO STUDY
THE WORD OF TRUTH.

Yield To Him.

Psalm 119:44
"So shall I keep thy law continually for ever and ever."

God knows that even though we are saved, we will still have failures.
**Our flesh is at war with the Spirit that now lives within us,
and sometimes the flesh gets the best of us.**

We must choose how we yield ourselves.

Romans 8:4-6
*"That the righteousness of the law might be fulfilled in us,
who walk not after the flesh, but after the Spirit. For they that are after
the flesh do mind the things of the flesh; but they that are after the
Spirit the things of the Spirit. For to be carnally minded is death;
but to be spiritually minded is life and peace."*

God does not expect us to live a perfect life.
He knows that is impossible for us to do. He simply desires for us to
live godly and righteously, striving to do our best for Him.

Philippians 3:14
*"I press toward the mark for the prize of the high calling of God
in Christ Jesus."*

The key is consistency.

We must be persuaded to constantly live according to the Word of Truth.

He is the Lamp unto our feet and the Light unto our path.

We need only seek, follow, and yield to Him as He leads, guides, and
directs us. The only way for us to live a life pleasing to God is to allow
the Word of Truth to live it through us.

For it is only through Him that we can truly live.

 **If we want the Lord
to order our steps,
we must consistently
yield to Him.**

WALK TOWARD LIBERTY.

Psalm 119:45
"And I will walk at liberty: for I seek thy precepts."

As we yield ourselves to the Lord, we begin to walk toward the liberty that is found in Him. We are free because of His sacrifice. Our sin was washed away by the precious blood of Jesus Christ the moment we placed our faith in His death, burial, and resurrection.

Galatians 5:1
"Stand fast therefore in the liberty wherewith Christ hath made us free, and be not entangled again with the yoke of bondage."

WALKING REQUIRES STEPS.

Each step we take can be ordered by the One that made it possible for us to walk with Him through His Word.

Psalm 37:23
"The steps of a good man are ordered by the Lord:
and he delighteth in his way."

We seek Him through His Word as a display of our love for Him. God so loved us that He sent His Son to give His life for us. The greatest way we can express our love for our Saviour is by giving our lives to the service of telling others about Him.

Share the love of Christ with those around you today.

Galatians 5:13
"For, brethren, ye have been called unto liberty;
only use not liberty for an occasion to the flesh,
but by love serve one another.
For all the law is fulfilled in one word, even in this;
Thou shalt love thy neighbour as thyself."

**IF WE WANT THE LORD
TO ORDER OUR STEPS,
WE MUST WALK TOWARD THE LIBERTY
THAT IS FOUND IN HIM.**

UNASHAMED.

Psalm 119:46
*"I will speak of thy testimonies also before kings,
and will not be ashamed."*

**Liberty in Christ Jesus not only makes us free,
it allows us to be bold and unashamed.**

Romans 1:16
*"For I am not ashamed of the gospel of Christ: for it is the power of
God unto salvation to every one that believeth;
to the Jew first, and also to the Greek."*

WHEN WE REMEMBER WHERE WE CAME FROM, WE TOO CAN BE UNASHAMED OF CHRIST AND HIS WORD.

Paul never forgot that he was *"a debtor"* who had experienced the power of God when he met Him on the road to Damascus. His life after that displayed his belief that if the Lord Jesus could save him, He could save anyone.

Philippians 1:20-21
"According to my earnest expectation and my hope, that in nothing I shall be ashamed, but that with all boldness, as always, so now also Christ shall be magnified in my body, whether it be by life, or by death. For to me to live is Christ, and to die is gain."

Paul was in prison when he pinned these Words, and even behind bars his priority was the glory of Christ. **He was so unashamed that he was even willing to die so that others may know the Lord.**

What a testimony Paul had,
and what an example he left for us to follow.

 IF WE WANT THE LORD
TO ORDER OUR STEPS,
WE MUST BE UNASHAMED
OF THE WORD OF GOD.

A Love For The Word.

Psalm 119:47
"And I will delight myself in thy commandments, which I have loved."

When we do not have a real love for something or someone, our desire to spend time with them will not be frequent or consistent.

If we do not truly love something, we will often neglect it or fail to appreciate its value.

Our relationship with the Lord is directly proportional to our love for His Word.

The Book of Psalms begins by describing a blessed man and how he conducts himself. Rather than spending time with those that hinder his walk with the Lord, he delights in the Word of God by deliberately making It a priority out of love.

Psalm 1:2-3
"But his delight is in the law of the LORD; and in his law doth he meditate day and night. And he shall be like a tree planted by the rivers of water, that bringeth forth his fruit in his season; his leaf also shall not wither; and whatsoever he doeth shall prosper."

The condition of our Bible will often reveal the condition of our heart. If It is rarely opened, the pages may become stiff or brittle. If It is used often, the leather will soften and the pages will display memories of time spent in the presence of the very One which inspired the Words to be pinned.

A love for the Word begins by delighting in the Scriptures.
Those that have come to know and love the Word of God desire to know and love the Scriptures more.

Psalm 119:97
"O how love I thy law! it is my meditation all the day."

If we want the Lord to order our steps, we must have a love for the Word.

Lift Our Hands.

Psalm 119:48
"My hands also will I lift up unto thy commandments,
which I have loved; and I will meditate in thy statutes."

Loving the Word will cause us to reach for the Word of God.
There is nothing like holding the Scriptures in our hands. We have
the choice to use our hands in honour of the God of the Bible.

Lifting Our Hands In Praise.
Within Scripture we read of people displaying their respect
and reverence to the Lord by raising their hands. May we also praise
Him as we read of what He has done for us through His Word.

Nehemiah 8:5-6
"And Ezra opened the book in the sight of all the people; (for he was
above all the people;) and when he opened it, all the people stood
up: And Ezra blessed the LORD, the great God. And all the people
answered, Amen, Amen, with lifting up their hands: and they bowed
their heads, and worshipped the LORD with their faces to the ground."

Lifting Our Hands In Practice.
Our faith is developed as we hear the Word of God,
but the Lord desires us to be more than hearers. Our hands enable
us to be a doer of the Word by putting our faith in action by doing
what the Bible says.

James 1:22,25
"But be ye doers of the word, and not hearers only, deceiving your
own selves...But whoso looketh into the perfect law of liberty, and
continueth therein, he being not a forgetful hearer, but a doer of the
work, this man shall be blessed in his deed."

Our hands have purpose to glorify the One Who created them.
We have the opportunity to share the Gospel using the hands that
God gave us. We can also spread His love by lending a hand to those
in need. **May we lift our hands for Him!**

IF WE WANT THE LORD
TO ORDER OUR STEPS,
WE MUST LIFT OUR HANDS FOR HIM!

HIS PROMISES.

Psalm 119:49
*"Remember the word unto thy servant,
upon which thou hast caused me to hope."*

**Sometimes we need a reminder that God is Faithful
to fulfill His promises.**

HE WILL NEVER GO BACK ON HIS WORD, BECAUSE HE CANNOT LIE.

Deuteronomy 7:9
*"Know therefore that the LORD thy God, he is God, the faithful God,
which keepeth covenant and mercy with them that love him and keep
his commandments to a thousand generations;"*

When it seems there is a delay in the fulfillment of His promise, He
has not failed us…for His timing is always right. We can find hope
within the trial, even when it feels like He is four days late.

1 Corinthians 10:13
*"There hath no temptation taken you but such as is common to man:
but God is faithful, who will not suffer you to be tempted above that
ye are able; but will with the temptation also make a way to escape,
that ye may be able to bear it."*

**When God promises something,
He will not only cause it to come to pass, but He will also enable us
to have faith that He will do it according to His will.**

Psalm 119:114
"Thou art my hiding place and my shield: I hope in thy word."

IF WE WANT THE LORD
TO ORDER OUR STEPS,
WE MUST CLING TO HIS PROMISES
THAT WE FIND WITHIN HIS WORD.

THE COMFORT OF THE SCRIPTURES.

Psalm 119:50
"This is my comfort in my affliction: for thy word hath quickened me."

**In the midst of affliction, it is only through
the Word of God that we can truly be comforted.**
It is not a matter of if we will face tribulation, but when; however, because of the Truth of God's Word, we can *"count it all joy"* because the Lord has promised that He will deliver us.

Psalm 34:19
*"Many are the afflictions of the righteous:
but the LORD delivereth him out of them all."*

Rather than allowing our trials to discourage and distract us, we can choose to shift our focus to the pages of Scripture. Within Them we can find the comfort that only the Word can give.

THE COMFORT OF THE SCRIPTURES GIVES US HOPE.
Romans 15:4
"For whatsoever things were written aforetime were written for our learning, that we through patience and comfort of the scriptures might have hope."

THE COMFORT OF THE SCRIPTURES GIVES US JOY.
Jeremiah 15:16
"Thy words were found, and I did eat them; and thy word was unto me the joy and rejoicing of mine heart: for I am called by thy name, O LORD God of hosts."

THE COMFORT OF THE SCRIPTURES GIVES US LIFE.
John 6:63
"It is the spirit that quickeneth; the flesh profiteth nothing: the words that I speak unto you, they are spirit, and they are life."

God's Word can give us hope, joy, life, and so much more. We need only seek comfort through each Word to find exactly what we need.

**IF WE WANT THE LORD
TO ORDER OUR STEPS,
WE MUST SEEK THE COMFORT OF THE
SCRIPTURES.**

Never Decline From The Word.

Psalm 119:51
"The proud have had me greatly in derision:
yet have I not declined from thy law."

Everyone struggles with something. Some people battle with pride bubbling up inside of them, while others cannot seem to get away from the distraction of prideful people.

Whatever keeps us *"greatly in derision"* is of our own choosing. We decide what we allow to affect our focus and purpose for the Lord. May we choose to lay aside every weight and sin that inhibits us from looking unto Jesus while running the race set before us.

Declining from God's Word cannot be an option.

We must never allow the fear of something, or someone, to keep us from doing what we know God has given us to do.

Psalm 118:5-6
"I called upon the LORD in distress: the LORD answered me,
and set me in a large place. The LORD is on my side; I will not fear:
what can man do unto me?"

Regardless of what distractions the devil puts in our way, we must decide to determine to finish well.

Acts 20:24
"But none of these things move me, neither count I my life dear unto
myself, so that I might finish my course with joy,
and the ministry, which I have received of the Lord Jesus,
to testify the gospel of the grace of God."

 If we want the Lord to order our steps, we must never decline from the Word of God.

MEMORIZE HIS WORD.

Psalm 119:52
*"I remembered thy judgments of old, O LORD;
and have comforted myself."*

When we take the time to remember what God has done for us in the past, it brings comfort in the present. He is the same God today as He was when He came through for us back then; and He is the same God that parted the Red Sea and fed the multitudes.
He never changes.

Hebrews 13:8
"Jesus Christ the same yesterday, and to day, and for ever."

REMEMBERING A VERSE OR PASSAGE FROM THE WORD OF GOD IS INVALUABLE IN THE TIME OF NEED.

We have the opportunity to hide the Word of God in our hearts.
**This helps us to not only apply the Word to our lives
but also to share the Scripture with others.**

MEMORIZING THE WORD WILL KEEP US FROM SIN.
Psalm 119:11
"Thy word have I hid in mine heart, that I might not sin against thee."

MEMORIZING THE WORD WILL ENABLE US TO SHARE.
1 Peter 3:15
"But sanctify the Lord God in your hearts: and be ready always to give an answer to every man that asketh you a reason of the hope that is in you with meekness and fear:"

THE MORE WE KNOW THE WORD OF GOD, THE MORE WE WILL LOVE THE GOD OF THE WORD.

One day we may have the freedom of reading the Word of God taken from us and we will be left with only those Scriptures that we have written upon our hearts.

**IF WE WANT THE LORD
TO ORDER OUR STEPS,
WE MUST MAKE AN EFFORT
TO MEMORIZE HIS WORD.**

FORSAKING THE WORD.

Psalm 119:53
*"Horror hath taken hold upon me
because of the wicked that forsake thy law."*

**It is a disheartening thing to see someone openly disobey
and forsake the Word of God.**
One could easily read this verse and think the Words do not apply
to them because they are saved; however, they have forgotten not
only where they came from, but also that they are still in the flesh and
capable of wickedness.

Matthew 7:3,5
*"And why beholdest thou the mote that is in thy brother's eye, but
considerest not the beam that is in thine own eye?...Thou hypocrite,
first cast out the beam out of thine own eye; and then shalt thou see
clearly to cast out the mote out of thy brother's eye."*

**Before we look down on someone else that is forsaking the Word
of God, we must consider how much we ourselves are guilty of the
same thing.** Instead of comparing ourselves with those around us,
we must only compare ourselves with the One Who spoke the verses
above, our Lord and Saviour, Jesus Christ.

**IT IS HIM WE ARE FORSAKING WHEN WE NEGLECT TO
SPEND TIME IN THE WORD OF GOD.**

How much does it affect us when we neglect the Word of God?
Job esteemed the Word of God as more than his necessary food.
When we go without a meal, our body is affected in different ways;
likewise, our spiritual condition is hindered when we neglect to feed
ourselves with the Scriptures.

Luke 4:3-4
*"And the devil said unto him, If thou be the Son of God, command
this stone that it be made bread. And Jesus answered him, saying,
It is written, That man shall not live by bread alone,
but by every word of God."*

**IF WE WANT THE LORD
TO ORDER OUR STEPS,
WE MUST NOT FORSAKE HIS WORD.**

SING HIS WORD.

Psalm 119:54
"Thy statutes have been my songs in the house of my pilgrimage."

While we are in this world, the Lord has given us His Word to sing as Songs in our heart on our way to Glory.

Psalm 89:1
"I will sing of the mercies of the LORD for ever: with my mouth will I make known thy faithfulness to all generations."

WE CAN CHOOSE TO PRAISE HIM WITH A SONG.

Psalm 28:7
"The LORD is my strength and my shield; my heart trusted in him, and I am helped: therefore my heart greatly rejoiceth; and with my song will I praise him."

God's Word can speak peace to us through Songs.
We must simply trust and obey Him as He guides and provides for our every need. Be not afraid today, Christian.
The Lord wants to be your Strength and Song.

Isaiah 12:2
"Behold, God is my salvation; I will trust, and not be afraid: for the LORD JEHOVAH is my strength and my song; he also is become my salvation."

Whether we can carry a tune or not, God has given us a Song to sing. Make a joyful noise unto Him today, and every day, through the testimony of His Word by singing with grace to the Lord.

Colossians 3:16
"Let the word of Christ dwell in you richly in all wisdom; teaching and admonishing one another in psalms and hymns and spiritual songs, singing with grace in your hearts to the Lord."

IF WE WANT THE LORD TO ORDER OUR STEPS, WE MUST SING HIS WORD.

REMEMBER.

Psalm 119:55
*"I have remembered thy name, O LORD,
in the night, and have kept thy law."*

WHILE WE READ THE WORD OF GOD,
WE MUST REMEMBER THE LORD OF THE WORD.
We must not only remember Him, we must remember His Name.

Psalm 34:3
"O magnify the LORD with me, and let us exalt his name together."

There is power in His Name, the power of salvation.

Acts 4:12
*"Neither is there salvation in any other: for there is none other name
under heaven given among men, whereby we must be saved."*

Salvation lies within our faith in the Name of Jesus and what He did
for us on Calvary. Where does our faith begin?

Romans 10:17
"So then faith cometh by hearing, and hearing by the word of God."

AS WE REMEMBER HIS NAME,
WE MUST ALSO REMEMBER HIS WORD,
FOR GOD MAGNIFIES HIS WORD EVEN ABOVE HIS NAME.

Psalm 138:2
*"I will worship toward thy holy temple,
and praise thy name for thy lovingkindness and for thy truth:
for thou hast magnified thy word above all thy name."*

At the Name of Jesus, the Name above every name, every knee shall
bow, and every tongue confess that Jesus Christ is Lord.
How much more powerful is His Word?

IF WE WANT THE LORD
TO ORDER OUR STEPS,
WE MUST REMEMBER HIS NAME
AND HIS WORD.

THE BENEFITS OF OBEYING.

Psalm 119:56
"This I had, because I kept thy precepts."

EVERYTHING WE HAVE
HAS BEEN GIVEN TO US FROM THE LORD.
His mercy and grace is evident all throughout our lives.

**All the benefits we have as God's children
are because of our obedience to His Word.**

Psalm 103:1-5
"Bless the LORD, O my soul: and all that is within me, bless his holy name. Bless the LORD, O my soul, and forget not all his benefits: Who forgiveth all thine iniquities; who healeth all thy diseases; Who redeemeth thy life from destruction; who crowneth thee with lovingkindness and tender mercies; Who satisfieth thy mouth with good things; so that thy youth is renewed like the eagle's."

Luke 12:24
"Consider the ravens: for they neither sow nor reap; which neither have storehouse nor barn; and God feedeth them: how much more are ye better than the fowls?"

The Lord cares for the birds, the flowers, and the grass;
how much more does He care for His children!
**We are not to think about what we need tomorrow,
but rather we must seek Him first and He will supply our needs.**

Matthew 6:33-34
"But seek ye first the kingdom of God, and his righteousness; and all these things shall be added unto you. Take therefore no thought for the morrow: for the morrow shall take thought for the things of itself. Sufficient unto the day is the evil thereof."

 IF WE WANT THE LORD
TO ORDER OUR STEPS,
WE MUST THANK HIM
FOR THE BENEFITS OF
OBEYING HIS WORD.

OUR PORTION.

Psalm 119:57
"Thou art my portion, O LORD:
I have said that I would keep thy words."

WE CAN CHOOSE THE WORD OF GOD AS OUR PORTION.
While many people choose to find their happiness in the things of this world, as God's children we have the unique opportunity to find our joy in Him through His Word.

WE CAN FIND HOPE IN HIS WORD.
Lamentations 3:24-26
"The LORD is my portion, saith my soul; therefore will I hope in him. The LORD is good unto them that wait for him, to the soul that seeketh him. It is good that a man should both hope and quietly wait for the salvation of the LORD."

WE CAN FIND STRENGTH IN HIS WORD.
Psalm 73:24-26
"Thou shalt guide me with thy counsel, and afterward receive me to glory. Whom have I in heaven but thee? and there is none upon earth that I desire beside thee. My flesh and my heart faileth: but God is the strength of my heart, and my portion for ever."

WE CAN FIND REFUGE IN HIS WORD.
Psalm 142:3-5
"When my spirit was overwhelmed within me, then thou knewest my path. In the way wherein I walked have they privily laid a snare for me. I looked on my right hand, and beheld, but there was no man that would know me: refuge failed me; no man cared for my soul. I cried unto thee, O Lord: I said, Thou art my refuge and my portion in the land of the living."

Whatever we need, His Word has the answer; we need only to seek Him to find it. While we wait, He is our Hope. When we are weak in faith, His strength will carry us through. When we are overwhelmed with the cares of this life, we can seek refuge in Him.

IF WE WANT THE LORD
TO ORDER OUR STEPS,
WE MUST CHOOSE HIS WORD
AS OUR PORTION.

Choose To Seek Him.

Psalm 119:58
*"I intreated thy favour with my whole heart:
be merciful unto me according to thy word."*

As we claim the Lord as our portion, we must also seek Him.
We must choose to seek Him not just when it's convenient, but with our whole heart. If we will seek the Lord, we will not return empty handed, for we are sure to find Him as the Word tells us. He is there, if only we will take the time to seek Him through His Word.

Seek Him before it is too late.
Isaiah 55:6-7
"Seek ye the LORD while he may be found, call ye upon him while he is near: Let the wicked forsake his way, and the unrighteous man his thoughts: and let him return unto the LORD, and he will have mercy upon him; and to our God, for he will abundantly pardon."

"be merciful unto me according to thy word."
The Psalmist pleaded that God would keep His promise.
We have read of God's promises
and will find Him faithful to keep them for us as well.

Seek His Mercy.
Psalm 51:1-3
"Have mercy upon me, O God, according to thy lovingkindness: according unto the multitude of thy tender mercies blot out my transgressions. Wash me throughly from mine iniquity, and cleanse me from my sin. For I acknowledge my transgressions: and my sin is ever before me."

If you need mercy today, seek His face and ask for it just as David did.
Make the choice to seek Him today, for He is waiting to be found.

Psalm 27:7-8
"Hear, O LORD, when I cry with my voice: have mercy also upon me, and answer me. When thou saidst, Seek ye my face; my heart said unto thee, Thy face, LORD, will I seek."

**If we want the Lord
to order our steps,
we must choose to seek Him
through His Word.**

Turn Our Feet.

Psalm 119:59
"I thought on my ways, and turned my feet unto thy testimonies."

How long has it been since we took the time
to ponder our behavior?
As we begin to think on our ways, we must first examine our hearts.
**The condition of our hearts is shown forth by our thoughts,
words, and actions.**

Matthew 15:18-19
*"But those things which proceed out of the mouth come forth from
the heart; and they defile the man.
For out of the heart proceed evil thoughts, murders, adulteries,
fornications, thefts, false witness, blasphemies:"*

A CLEAN HEART IS A SIMPLE AND SINCERE PRAYER AWAY.
If we will confess our sins, the Lord is not only Faithful and Just to
forgive us but also to cleanse our hearts to be more like Him.
If we desire to live pure, we must keep our hearts pure.

Proverbs 4:23
"Keep thy heart with all diligence; for out of it are the issues of life."

As our hearts become clean, we will desire to change how we think,
what we say, and where we go. Our surroundings have the greatest
affect on our thoughts and actions.
WHERE WILL YOUR FEET TAKE YOU TODAY?

Proverbs 4:26
"Ponder the path of thy feet, and let all thy ways be established."

**After the Psalmist thought about the ways of his heart,
he turned his feet toward the Word of God.**

Proverbs 16:3
*"Commit thy works unto the LORD,
and thy thoughts shall be established."*

 **IF WE WANT THE LORD
TO ORDER OUR STEPS,
WE MUST TURN OUR FEET
TOWARD HIS WORD.**

WE MUST NOT DELAY.

Psalm 119:60
"I made haste, and delayed not to keep thy commandments."

Procrastination is an easy attribute to develop.
**WE OFTEN PUT OFF UNTIL TOMORROW
WHAT GOD HAS MEANT FOR US TO DO TODAY.**

James 4:14-15
*"Whereas ye know not what shall be on the morrow.
For what is your life? It is even a vapour, that appeareth for a little
time, and then vanisheth away. For that ye ought to say,
If the Lord will, we shall live, and do this, or that."*

If we feel conviction of unconfessed sin, we should confess it now for
"he is faithful and just to forgive us our sins". 1 John 1:9

If we feel a calling to do something for the Lord, we should answer
the call immediately, *"For the gifts and callings of God are without
repentance."* Romans 11:29

Make haste in salvation. After the great earthquake, the Philippian
Jailor asked Paul and Silas what he needed to do to be saved. They
were quick to respond, and the jailor was quick to repent.

**WHEN WE HAVE THE OPPORTUNITY TO SHARE THE
GOSPEL, WE CANNOT DELAY FOR ETERNITY IS AT STAKE.**

Acts 16:30-31
*"And brought them out, and said, Sirs, what must I do to be saved?
And they said, Believe on the Lord Jesus Christ,
and thou shalt be saved, and thy house."*

Make haste in taking the next step.
Regardless of what our next step in our walk with the Lord is, when
He speaks to us, we must make haste to obey Him.
Sometimes the next step is unclear, but we can *"Trust in the Lord…
and he shall direct our paths."* Proverbs 3:5-6

**IF WE WANT THE LORD
TO ORDER OUR STEPS,
WE MUST NOT DELAY
TO OBEY HIS WORD.**

BEWARE OF THE DANGER.

Psalm 119:61
*"The bands of the wicked have robbed me:
but I have not forgotten thy law."*

It may seem as though many are against us,
and they very well may be, but no matter who or what stands against
us, we can rest in the Truth of God's Word.

IT IS IN TIMES OF TROUBLE
THAT WE NEED TO REMEMBER THE WORD THE MOST,
FOR HIS PROMISES ARE TRUE!

Ephesians 2:8-9
*"For by grace are ye saved through faith; and that not of yourselves:
it is the gift of God: Not of works, lest any man should boast."*

We are only saved because of the grace of God. From the air that we
breathe to the shoes on our feet, the roof over our head, the food on
our table, the pillow we lay our head on at night, and on and on and
on. The blessings that we have are not our doing. Every thing that
we have is from the Lord. When we fail to remember that everything
comes from Him, we are in dangerous territory.

THERE IS DANGER IN FORGETTING THE WORD OF GOD.
Deuteronomy 8:19
*"And it shall be, if thou do at all forget the LORD thy God, and walk
after other gods, and serve them, and worship them, I testify against
you this day that ye shall surely perish."*

John 15:5
*"I am the vine, ye are the branches: He that abideth in me,
and I in him, the same bringeth forth much fruit:
for without me ye can do nothing."*

We must remember that we are nothing without Him.

IF WE WANT THE LORD
TO ORDER OUR STEPS,
WE MUST BEWARE OF THE DANGER
OF FORGETTING THE WORD OF GOD.

THANK HIM EVEN IN THE NIGHT.

Psalm 119:62
*"At midnight I will rise to give thanks unto thee
because of thy righteous judgments."*

GOD'S WORD TEACHES US TO GIVE THANKS UNTO THE LORD EVEN IN THE NIGHT HOURS.

Psalm 63:6
*"When I remember thee upon my bed,
and meditate on thee in the night watches."*

Paul and Silas showed us that even when we feel as if we are in a dark prison, we can pray to give thanks and praise unto God. Doing so will also be a witness to those around us.

Acts 16:25
"And at midnight Paul and Silas prayed, and sang praises unto God: and the prisoners heard them."

The more we pray, the more we will have to be thankful for.

Philippians 4:6
"Be careful for nothing; but in every thing by prayer and supplication with thanksgiving let your requests be made known unto God."

As we walk with the Lord, we can best show our faith in Him by being thankful in every circumstance, resting in the Truth that He does all things well. A thankful heart abounds with thanksgiving for Him and His Word.

Colossians 2:6-7
"As ye have therefore received Christ Jesus the Lord, so walk ye in him: Rooted and built up in him, and stablished in the faith, as ye have been taught, abounding therein with thanksgiving."

IF WE WANT THE LORD
TO ORDER OUR STEPS,
WE MUST THANK HIM EVEN
IN THE NIGHT HOURS OF OUR LIVES.

Our Companions.

Psalm 119:63
*"I am a companion of all them that fear thee,
and of them that keep thy precepts."*

The Company We Keep Is Important.

The phrase, "you are who you hang around", is very true. Who we choose to be our friends, mentors, and especially our spouse sets the course for who we will become.

Proverbs 9:10
*"The fear of the LORD is the beginning of wisdom:
and the knowledge of the holy is understanding."*

As much as it is wise to fear the Lord, it is also wise to surround ourselves with people whose lives display a fear of the Lord.

Proverbs 13:20
*"He that walketh with wise men shall be wise:
but a companion of fools shall be destroyed."*

When needing advice, we must seek out godly counsel in order to make our decision in light of what the Bible says. Sometimes a trustworthy godly friend can offer a new perspective that perhaps we did not see beforehand.

Proverbs 27:9
*"Ointment and perfume rejoice the heart:
so doth the sweetness of a man's friend by hearty counsel."*

The friend who has a close walk with the Lord will encourage us to walk closer with Him ourselves. Being able to share what the Lord has given in time spent with Him is a priceless gift from God.

**Thank the Lord today for the godly friends in your life,
for they are blessings from Him.**

 **If We Want The Lord
To Order Our Steps,
We Must Choose
Our Companions Wisely.**

DESIRE TO LEARN.

Psalm 119:64
"The earth, O LORD, is full of thy mercy: teach me thy statutes."

The more we encounter the Word of God, the more we will see the Truth of God's Word all around us.

THIS BEGINS WITH A DESIRE TO LEARN THE TRUTH OF THE WORD OF GOD.

Psalm 27:11-14
"Teach me thy way, O LORD, and lead me in a plain path, because of mine enemies. Deliver me not over unto the will of mine enemies: for false witnesses are risen up against me, and such as breathe out cruelty. I had fainted, unless I had believed to see the goodness of the LORD in the land of the living. Wait on the LORD: be of good courage, and he shall strengthen thine heart: wait, I say, on the LORD."

In the midst of the darkness of this wicked world, God's mercy abounds. With His mercy, comes His goodness and His grace. Those that experience the mercy of God only desire to know and obey Him more. We have the opportunity to rest in Him while He teaches us.

Matthew 11:28-29
"Come unto me, all ye that labour and are heavy laden, and I will give you rest. Take my yoke upon you, and learn of me; for I am meek and lowly in heart: and ye shall find rest unto your souls."

THE MORE WE LEARN THE WORD OF GOD, THE MORE WE WILL BE PREPARED TO SPEAK HIS WORD.

Isaiah 50:4
"The Lord GOD hath given me the tongue of the learned, that I should know how to speak a word in season to him that is weary: he wakeneth morning by morning, he wakeneth mine ear to hear as the learned."

IF WE WANT THE LORD TO ORDER OUR STEPS, WE MUST DESIRE TO LEARN THE TRUTH FROM HIS WORD.

PRAY MORE OFTEN.

Psalm 119:65
*"Thou hast dealt well with thy servant, O LORD,
according unto thy word."*

Here we see the result to a prayer the Psalmist had prayed earlier in the chapter: *"Deal bountifully with thy servant, that I may live, and keep thy word."* Psalm 119:17

HE HAD SEEN THE LORD ANSWER HIS PRAYER.
When we see God's hand in a situation that we have brought to His throne of grace, it should encourage us to pray more often.

Hebrews 4:16
"Let us therefore come boldly unto the throne of grace, that we may obtain mercy, and find grace to help in time of need."

GOD ALWAYS ANSWERS EVERY PRAYER WE PRAY.
There are three types of answers that God gives to our prayers. Sometimes He says "yes" sometimes He says "no",
and sometimes His answer is "wait".

Matthew 7:7-8
"Ask, and it shall be given you; seek, and ye shall find; knock, and it shall be opened unto you: For every one that asketh receiveth; and he that seeketh findeth; and to him that knocketh it shall be opened."

The Word of God tells us that He will answer.

Imagine what we could be given…imagine what we could find…imagine what could be opened unto us…if only we would ask, seek, and knock. Great and mighty things await those who call upon Him.

Jeremiah 33:3
"Call unto me, and I will answer thee, and shew thee great and mighty things, which thou knowest not."

**IF WE WANT THE LORD
TO ORDER OUR STEPS,
WE MUST PRAY MORE OFTEN.**

PRAY BEFORE WE READ.

Psalm 119:66
"Teach me good judgment and knowledge:
for I have believed thy commandments."

We can read the Word just to read; or we can pray before we read, asking God to teach us as we read. When we pray, the Lord will answer; and unlike other requests, when we ask the Lord to teach us from His Word, He always says, "Yes!"

Psalm 34:10
"The young lions do lack, and suffer hunger:
but they that seek the LORD shall not want any good thing."

AS WE PRAY BEFORE WE READ,
WE MUST BELIEVE THAT WHAT WE WILL READ IS TRUE.

It is impossible for God to lie, so therefore every single Word within the Word of God is the Truth. When we come to the Scriptures with our hearts believing the God of the Word, we will never be disappointed. He is always able to show us something new.

2 Timothy 1:12
"For the which cause I also suffer these things:
nevertheless I am not ashamed: for I know whom I have believed, and
am persuaded that he is able to keep that which I have committed
unto him against that day."

Jesus prayed to God the Father for us to be sanctified through His Word. As we read, God will answer both the Lord Jesus' prayers and ours for us to learn the Truth.

John 17:17-19
"Sanctify them through thy truth: thy word is truth. As thou hast sent
me into the world, even so have I also sent them into the world. And
for their sakes I sanctify myself, that they also might be sanctified
through the truth."

IF WE WANT THE LORD
TO ORDER OUR STEPS,
WE MUST PRAY BEFORE WE READ.

WHEN WE GO ASTRAY.

Psalm 119:67
"Before I was afflicted I went astray: but now have I kept thy word."

THE WEAKNESS OF OUR FLESH
CAN CAUSE US TO GO ASTRAY.

We can go far down the wrong road before we even realize we have wandered from that which is right.

Isaiah 53:6
"All we like sheep have gone astray; we have turned every one to his own way; and the LORD hath laid on him the iniquity of us all."

That day on the Cross, Jesus Christ bore the weight of the sins of every human being that had ever been or will be born. Though we may stray, because of our faith in what He did for us on Calvary, we are not forsaken.

Matthew 18:12-13
"How think ye? if a man have an hundred sheep, and one of them be gone astray, doth he not leave the ninety and nine, and goeth into the mountains, and seeketh that which is gone astray? And if so be that he find it, verily I say unto you, he rejoiceth more of that sheep, than of the ninety and nine which went not astray."

The Good Shepherd desires to find us and show us our need for correction. When we do not see this necessity on our own, He must intervene by chastisement. Through affliction, we can learn where we are spiritually, and repent...or begin to turn ourselves back toward the right direction.

Proverbs 3:11-12
"My son, despise not the chastening of the LORD; neither be weary of his correction: For whom the LORD loveth he correcteth; even as a father the son in whom he delighteth."

He loves us. When we feel His chastening hand and turn, we too can say..."*but now have I kept thy word.*"

**IF WE WANT THE LORD
TO ORDER OUR STEPS,
WE MUST TURN BACK
WHEN WE GO ASTRAY.**

GOD IS GOOD.

Psalm 119:68
"Thou art good, and doest good; teach me thy statutes."

EVEN IN AFFLICTION, GOD IS GOOD.
We must realize that though we are afflicted, we can trust Him that it is for our good, because He is Good.
It may seem simple, but through it all...God is Good.

Job 13:15
*"Though he slay me, yet will I trust in him:
but I will maintain mine own ways before him."*

God is Good...because He is Trustworthy.
Psalm 34:8
*"O taste and see that the LORD is good:
blessed is the man that trusteth in him."*

God is Good...because He is Forgiving.
Psalm 86:5
*"For thou, Lord, art good, and ready to forgive;
and plenteous in mercy unto all them that call upon thee."*

God is Good...because He is Merciful.
Psalm 106:1
*"Praise ye the LORD. O give thanks unto the LORD; for he is good:
for his mercy endureth for ever."*

God is Good...because He is a Refuge.
Nahum 1:7
*"The LORD is good, a strong hold in the day of trouble;
and he knoweth them that trust in him."*

Through it all...God is Good.

IF WE WANT THE LORD
TO ORDER OUR STEPS,
WE MUST REMEMBER
THAT GOD IS GOOD.

STAND STILL.

Psalm 119:69
*"The proud have forged a lie against me:
but I will keep thy precepts with my whole heart."*

The best way to answer those who have something to say about us is by faithfully living our lives devoted to the Lord and His Word.
LET OUR ACTIONS SPEAK LOUDER THAN THEIR WORDS.

When the Children of Israel murmured to Moses after he led them out of Egypt and into the wilderness, he responded with the Lord's advice to both them and us today.

Exodus 14:13-14
*"And Moses said unto the people,
Fear ye not, stand still, and see the salvation of the LORD, which he will shew to you to day: for the Egyptians whom ye have seen to day, ye shall see them again no more for ever. The LORD shall fight for you, and ye shall hold your peace."*

The children of Israel saw no way for the Lord to intervene in their situation. The Lord then gave Moses the instructions for how He would fight for them, making a way where there was no way.
He spoke the Answer to their problem.

Exodus 14:15-16
"And the LORD said unto Moses, Wherefore criest thou unto me? speak unto the children of Israel, that they go forward: But lift thou up thy rod, and stretch out thine hand over the sea, and divide it: and the children of Israel shall go on dry ground through the midst of the sea."

The rod that Moses lifted up and stretched out over the sea in front of them was the instrument that God used for the people to see the Lord's power to deliver them. Today, we also have a Rod that God uses to speak to us and show us the Answer.
The Word of God divides our problems.

**IF WE WANT THE LORD
TO ORDER OUR STEPS,
WE MUST STAND STILL
AND ALLOW HIM TO FIGHT FOR US.**

CHOOSE THE WORD.

Psalm 119:70
"Their heart is as fat as grease; but I delight in thy law."

Those whose *"heart is as fat as grease"* have only the things of this world in their view. **God hates a carnal heart and mind.**

Romans 8:5-8
"For they that are after the flesh do mind the things of the flesh; but they that are after the Spirit the things of the Spirit. For to be carnally minded is death; but to be spiritually minded is life and peace. Because the carnal mind is enmity against God: for it is not subject to the law of God, neither indeed can be. So then they that are in the flesh cannot please God."

When we mind the things of the flesh…
We allow ourselves to become insensitive to the Word of God.
2 Timothy 3:7-8
"Ever learning, and never able to come to the knowledge of the truth. Now as Jannes and Jambres withstood Moses, so do these also resist the truth: men of corrupt minds, reprobate concerning the faith."

We become ignorant to the sin in our lives.
Ephesians 4:18-19
"Having the understanding darkened, being alienated from the life of God through the ignorance that is in them, because of the blindness of their heart: Who being past feeling have given themselves over unto lasciviousness, to work all uncleanness with greediness."

INSTEAD OF ALLOWING OUR HEARTS TO BE FILLED WITH GREASE, WE CAN CHOOSE THE WORD OVER THE WORLD.

"…but I delight in thy law."
The Word within our hearts will create in us the desire to do what is pleasing to God. When He directs us, we cannot fail.

Psalm 37:31
"The law of his God is in his heart; none of his steps shall slide."

**IF WE WANT THE LORD
TO ORDER OUR STEPS,
WE MUST CHOOSE THE WORD
OVER THE WORLD.**

THE PURPOSE OF AFFLICTION.

Psalm 119:71
"It is good for me that I have been afflicted;
that I might learn thy statutes."

What a testimony to have during our trials! How we endure affliction speaks volumes of our faith. We too can say this when we remember that all the things the Lord does work together for our good.

Romans 8:28
"And we know that all things work together for good to them that love God, to them who are the called according to his purpose."

It is through affliction, we are able to learn more of the truths in God's Word that we would not fully understand otherwise. The promises and truths found in the Scriptures become more real to us as we see God work each of them to be true within our lives.

We will find that the Lord is near the brokenhearted, and He is Faithful to deliver His children out of every affliction.

Psalm 34:18-19
"The LORD is nigh unto them that are of a broken heart; and saveth such as be of a contrite spirit. Many are the afflictions of the righteous: but the LORD delivereth him out of them all."

THOUGH OUR AFFLICTIONS ARE MANY, THEY GIVE US THE OPPORTUNITY TO SEE THE BEAUTY OF THE LORD AND GIVE HIM THE GLORY THROUGH THE SUFFERING.

As Christians, we will suffer affliction and persecution.
The Bible tells us that our days are few and full of trouble, but we must remember that the pain we feel here is only temporary.

2 Corinthians 4:17
"For our light affliction, which is but for a moment, worketh for us a far more exceeding and eternal weight of glory;"

IF WE WANT THE LORD
TO ORDER OUR STEPS,
WE MUST FOCUS ON THE
PURPOSE OF AFFLICTION
INSTEAD OF THE PAIN.

THE WORD IS BETTER.

Psalm 119:72
*"The law of thy mouth is better unto me
than thousands of gold and silver."*

We tend to seek counsel, encouragement, and pleasure from the people and things around us. David knew from experience that he could find all these things and more within the Scriptures.
He knew that the Word is better than anything money could buy.

Psalm 19:7-11
"The law of the LORD is perfect, converting the soul: the testimony of the LORD is sure, making wise the simple. The statutes of the LORD are right, rejoicing the heart: the commandment of the LORD is pure, enlightening the eyes. The fear of the LORD is clean, enduring for ever: the judgments of the LORD are true and righteous altogether. More to be desired are they than gold, yea, than much fine gold: sweeter also than honey and the honeycomb. Moreover by them is thy servant warned: and in keeping of them there is great reward."

WISDOM IS FOUND WITHIN THE WORD OF GOD.
He desires to make us wise through our learning of the Scriptures.

Proverbs 8:11
*"For wisdom is better than rubies; and all the things
that may be desired are not to be compared to it."*

DAVID HAD HIS THOUSANDS OF GOLD AND SILVER, YET HE ESTEEMED THE WORD OF GOD ABOVE ALL HIS RICHES.

**He willingly suffered affliction because it caused him
to understand the Truth of the Scriptures better.**

IF WE WANT THE LORD
TO ORDER OUR STEPS,
WE MUST ACKNOWLEDGE
THAT THE WORD IS BETTER
THAN ANYTHING WE COULD DESIRE.

OUR CREATOR'S WORD.

Psalm 119:73
*"Thy hands have made me and fashioned me:
give me understanding, that I may learn thy commandments."*

Before sin entered into the world, God made us in His image.
We were fashioned from dust after His likeness,
as He breathed life into Adam.

Genesis 2:7
*"And the LORD God formed man of the dust of the ground,
and breathed into his nostrils the breath of life;
and man became a living soul."*

HE CREATED US FOR HIS GLORY AND REDEEMED US SO THAT WE COULD FELLOWSHIP WITH HIM THROUGH HIS WORD.

Isaiah 43:1,7
*"But now thus saith the LORD that created thee, O Jacob, and he
that formed thee, O Israel, Fear not: for I have redeemed thee, I have
called thee by thy name; thou art mine...Even every one that is called
by my name: for I have created him for my glory, I have formed him;
yea, I have made him."*

OUR CREATOR EVEN GIVES US THE DESIRE TO UNDERSTAND MORE OF HIS WORD.

Just as He breathed life into us, He divinely breathed His Word into
this world so that His creation could be complete in Him.

2 Timothy 3:16-17
*"All scripture is given by inspiration of God,
and is profitable for doctrine, for reproof, for correction,
for instruction in righteousness: That the man of God may be perfect,
thoroughly furnished unto all good works."*

IF WE WANT THE LORD TO ORDER OUR STEPS, WE MUST SEEK TO UNDERSTAND OUR CREATOR'S WORD.

HOPE IN HIS WORD.

Psalm 119:74
*"They that fear thee will be glad when they see me;
because I have hoped in thy word."*

When the circumstances of life get us down and it seems as if no hope can be found, there is hope in His Word. **Whatever our situation, His Word has the Answer, for He is the Answer.**

HOPE FOR OUR SALVATION.
Psalm 119:81
"My soul fainteth for thy salvation: but I hope in thy word."

HOPE FOR OUR SAFETY.
Psalm 119:114
"Thou art my hiding place and my shield: I hope in thy word."

HOPE FOR OUR SORROW.
Psalm 119:147
*"I prevented the dawning of the morning, and cried:
I hoped in thy word."*

We are justified by our faith in Jesus Christ, and our faith in Him brings us hope for His glory during the trials we face.

Romans 5:1-2
"Therefore being justified by faith, we have peace with God through our Lord Jesus Christ: By whom also we have access by faith into this grace wherein we stand, and rejoice in hope of the glory of God."

AS WE HOPE IN HIS WORD, WE CAN REST IN HIM WHILE WE WAIT FOR HIM TO LEAD, GUIDE, AND DIRECT US.

Psalm 130:5
"I wait for the Lord, my soul doth wait, and in his word do I hope."

 **IF WE WANT THE LORD
TO ORDER OUR STEPS,
WE MUST HOPE IN HIS WORD.**

KNOW HIS WORD.

Psalm 119:75
*"I know, O LORD, that thy judgments are right,
and that thou in faithfulness hast afflicted me."*

In the midst of our affliction, we have to decide whether to allow the circumstances to distract us or to remind us of what God's Word says. **He brings situations to pass so that we can learn Who He is in the middle of our suffering.**

Psalm 119:7
"I will praise thee with uprightness of heart, when I shall have learned thy righteous judgments."

UNLESS WE KNOW HIS WORD, WE CANNOT GIVE HIM THE PRAISE HE DESERVES.
Our hearts cannot be right with Him if we are not spending time in the Scriptures. Studying the Word shows us Who God is and why He alone deserves our praise.

Psalm 119:128
"Therefore I esteem all thy precepts concerning all things to be right; and I hate every false way."

UNLESS WE KNOW HIS WORD, WE CANNOT UNDERSTAND THE DIFFERENCE BETWEEN RIGHT AND WRONG.
In order to know which way is wrong, we must first know the right way. Jesus Christ alone is the Way, the Truth, and the Life. **We cannot be on the right way, have the Truth, or experience real life without Him.**

ALL OF THIS BEGINS WITH KNOWING HIS WORD.
Before we praise the Lord, we must know why He deserves our praise. Before we thank the Lord, we must know what He has done for us. Before we stand for God, we must know what is right.

IF WE WANT THE LORD TO ORDER OUR STEPS, WE MUST BEGIN BY SEEKING TO KNOW HIS WORD.

ASK ACCORDING TO HIS WORD.

Psalm 119:76
*"Let, I pray thee, thy merciful kindness be for my comfort,
according to thy word unto thy servant."*

He had read or heard God's Word before. He knew what the Word of God said, and he was praying in faith for the Lord's *"merciful kindness"* to be his comfort because he had heard It to be true!

Romans 10:17
"So then faith cometh by hearing, and hearing by the word of God."

**When we know God's Word,
we can then pray according to His Word...**

ASKING WHILE BELIEVING THAT HE IS ABLE.
Matthew 21:22
*"And all things, whatsoever ye shall ask in prayer,
believing, ye shall receive."*

ASKING IN HIS NAME.
John 16:24
*"Hitherto have ye asked nothing in my name:
ask, and ye shall receive, that your joy may be full."*

ASKING IN FAITH.
James 1:6
*"But let him ask in faith, nothing wavering. For he that wavereth is like
a wave of the sea driven with the wind and tossed."*

ASKING WHILE OBEYING.
1 John 3:22
*"And whatsoever we ask, we receive of him, because we keep his
commandments, and do those things that are pleasing in his sight."*

**His Word has the answer because He is the Answer...we need only
ask Him according to His Word.** He will not only answer, but He will
also comfort, direct, guide, and provide for us.

**IF WE WANT THE LORD
TO ORDER OUR STEPS,
WE MUST ASK
ACCORDING TO HIS WORD.**

LIVING IN THE WORD.

Psalm 119:77
"Let thy tender mercies come unto me, that I may live:
for thy law is my delight."

We cannot truly live without God's Word being made manifest in our lives. It is by the Lord's mercy and grace that we are able to come unto Him.

LIVING IN THE WORD RELEASES
GOD'S BLESSINGS IN OUR LIVES.
Psalm 119:17
"Deal bountifully with thy servant, that I may live, and keep thy word."

LIVING IN THE WORD REMITS GOD'S MERCY IN OUR LIVES.
Psalm 119:77
"Let thy tender mercies come unto me, that I may live:
for thy law is my delight."

LIVING IN THE WORD RELAYS
GOD'S STRENGTH IN OUR LIVES.
Psalm 119:116
"Uphold me according unto thy word, that I may live:
and let me not be ashamed of my hope."

Life begins by hearing and believing the Word of God.

We have the great responsibility to tell others
that everlasting life is only found in Jesus Christ.
Without Him, we are condemned to death.

John 5:24
"Verily, verily, I say unto you, He that heareth my word, and believeth
on him that sent me, hath everlasting life, and shall not come into
condemnation; but is passed from death unto life."

IF WE WANT THE LORD
TO ORDER OUR STEPS,
WE MUST BEGIN BY
LIVING IN THE WORD OF GOD.

PRAY FOR OUR ENEMIES.

Psalm 119:78
"Let the proud be ashamed; for they dealt perversely with me without a cause: but I will meditate in thy precepts."

EVEN IN OUR SERVICE FOR THE LORD, WE WILL HAVE ENEMIES.

Jesus had them, and He was without sin. If Christ was not without enemies, how can we think we wouldn't have them? **Thankfully, Jesus Himself told us how to deal with those people.**

Matthew 5:43-44
"Ye have heard that it hath been said, Thou shalt love thy neighbour, and hate thine enemy. But I say unto you, Love your enemies, bless them that curse you, do good to them that hate you, and pray for them which despitefully use you, and persecute you;"

In the middle of His Sermon on the Mount, Jesus told the multitudes of people how to react when confronted by their enemies. Some of His enemies may have even been with them in the same crowd that intently listened as He compassionately spoke to them that day.

When we pray for those that have wronged us, we receive both the blessing of obeying the Lord's command and receiving the absence of bitterness. How can we be bitter if we ask for the Lord's help in the situation? Bitterness begins to grow when we talk to others about the problem instead of taking it to the Lord.

Jesus Christ prayed for His enemies even while they crucified Him.
Luke 23:34

Stephen prayed for those who threw the rocks that caused his death.
Acts 7:59-60

We can become bitter at the stone throwers or better by choosing to pray for them while spending time in the Word. When we pray for those that have *"dealt perversely"* with us, we become closer to the One Who wants to fight for us.

IF WE WANT THE LORD TO ORDER OUR STEPS, WE MUST PRAY FOR OUR ENEMIES.

GODLY PEOPLE.

Psalm 119:79
*"Let those that fear thee turn unto me,
and those that have known thy testimonies."*

The Psalmist also prayed that God would bless his life with Godly People. His request was even specific that they know the testimonies of the Word of God.

Ecclesiastes 4:9-10
"Two are better than one; because they have a good reward for their labour. For if they fall, the one will lift up his fellow: but woe to him that is alone when he falleth; for he hath not another to help him up."

We should also desire to pray for our lives to be surrounded by Godly people. We can be more effective for the cause of Christ when we serve together with Godly people.

GODLY CORRECTION.
Proverbs 27:6
A Godly friend or family member will not always agree with everything that we do. We need people who will caution us of any wrongdoing they see creeping into our lives.

GODLY COUNSEL.
Proverbs 27:9
We must not seek counsel from the things of the world but rather of the Word. When we receive Biblical advice from someone who cares about us, it makes our heart rejoice!

GODLY CONVERSATION.
Proverbs 27:17
Our lives need sharpened by the Sword of the Word of God. There are few things sweeter than a discussion among friends centered on the Word of God and what our Saviour has done for us.

IF WE WANT THE LORD
TO ORDER OUR STEPS,
WE MUST SURROUND OURSELVES
WITH GODLY PEOPLE.

FILL OUR HEARTS.

Psalm 119:80
"Let my heart be sound in thy statutes; that I be not ashamed."

OUR HEARTS CANNOT BE COMPLETE WITHOUT THE WORD OF GOD.

The void that we sometimes feel within ourselves can only be filled by the Lord and His Word.

Psalm 18:30-32
"As for God, his way is perfect: the word of the LORD is tried: he is a buckler to all those that trust in him. For who is God save the LORD? or who is a rock save our God? It is God that girdeth me with strength, and maketh my way perfect."

We must daily fill our hearts with the Word of God because we cannot stand on our own. He can make our way perfect because His Way is perfect. Each time we apply the Truths of God's Word to our hearts, we are strengthened by His strength.

Psalm 19:7
"The law of the LORD is perfect, converting the soul: the testimony of the LORD is sure, making wise the simple."

The Word of God converts our souls by discerning our thoughts and intentions. We must not be satisfied with only a form of godliness, when God is offering His power to us through the Truth of His Word.

Hebrews 4:12
"For the word of God is quick, and powerful, and sharper than any twoedged sword, piercing even to the dividing asunder of soul and spirit, and of the joints and marrow, and is a discerner of the thoughts and intents of the heart."

 IF WE WANT THE LORD
TO ORDER OUR STEPS,
WE MUST FILL OUR HEARTS
WITH HIS WORD.

RENEW OURSELVES.

Psalm 119:81
"My soul fainteth for thy salvation: but I hope in thy word."

As our soul begins to show the weakness of our flesh, we can choose to strengthen our faith through His Word. Hope begins with faith, and without faith it is impossible to please God.

Isaiah 40:31
"But they that wait upon the LORD shall renew their strength; they shall mount up with wings as eagles; they shall run, and not be weary; and they shall walk, and not faint."

WHEN WE WAIT UPON HIM THROUGH HIS WORD, HE RENEWS HIS STRENGTH IN US.
As we yield to His strength, we can walk with Him and run for Him.

2 Corinthians 4:16-18
"For which cause we faint not; but though our outward man perish, yet the inward man is renewed day by day. For our light affliction, which is but for a moment, worketh for us a far more exceeding and eternal weight of glory; While we look not at the things which are seen, but at the things which are not seen: for the things which are seen are temporal; but the things which are not seen are eternal."

WE MUST RENEW OURSELVES DAILY BY SPENDING TIME WITH THE LORD THROUGH HIS WORD.
Renewed strength and growth will only come as we die to our own will and take up our cross for His glory.

Luke 9:23-24
"And he said to them all, If any man will come after me, let him deny himself, and take up his cross daily, and follow me. For whosoever will save his life shall lose it: but whosoever will lose his life for my sake, the same shall save it."

Denying our will leads to following His.

 **IF WE WANT THE LORD TO ORDER OUR STEPS, WE MUST RENEW OURSELVES DAILY THROUGH HIS WORD.**

WAIT ON HIS TIMING.

Psalm 119:82
"Mine eyes fail for thy word, saying, When wilt thou comfort me?"

OUR TIMING IS RARELY GOD'S TIMING.
We tend to want things to happen immediately or when we feel is convenient for us, but God does not work that way. We see within His Word time and time again where He chooses to make His people wait until He sees fit for things to happen.

The usual example of God's timing is when Jesus raised Lazarus from the dead after arriving four days late according to his sisters. More often than not we can relate with how Mary and Martha felt. Just when we think all hope is gone is when God usually begins to reveal to us that He had been working behind the scenes all along.

When? - A Lack of Patience
Impatience is one of our biggest weaknesses. Waiting is not fun, and it is easy to give up hope or quit praying for God to move. When God makes us wait, He always has something better on the way.

Hebrews 10:35-36
"Cast not away therefore your confidence, which hath great recompence of reward. For ye have need of patience, that, after ye have done the will of God, ye might receive the promise."

When? - A Longing for Provision
The mature Christian has learned that impatience must grow into longsuffering, which comes by yielding to the Holy Spirit as He works within us.

Regardless of our reasoning for asking "When?" we must remember Who we are waiting on. He is working all things for our good and His glory. **We must wait by placing our faith in Him.**

Psalm 39:7
"And now, Lord, what wait I for? my hope is in thee."

IF WE WANT THE LORD
TO ORDER OUR STEPS,
WE MUST WAIT ON HIS TIMING.

NEGLECTING THE WORD.

Psalm 119:83
*"For I am become like a bottle in the smoke;
yet do I not forget thy statutes."*

During the time this Psalm was penned, bottles were made of animal skin and dried by smoke. For the Psalmist to describe himself as such a bottle, he must have been in a very uncomfortable state. Despite a lack of comfort, he made sure not to forget about the Word of God.

When we find ourselves in an uncomfortable situation,
we tend to rely on anyone or anything to rescue us.
God's Word has the Answer to soothe our soul.

Proverbs 3:1-3
"My son, forget not my law; but let thine heart keep my commandments: For length of days, and long life, and peace, shall they add to thee. Let not mercy and truth forsake thee: bind them about thy neck; write them upon the table of thine heart:"

WE OFTEN TAKE FOR GRANTED THE BENEFITS OF MAKING THE WORD OF GOD A PRIORITY IN OUR LIVES.

Our impatience causes us to ask God, *"When wilt thou comfort me?"* Yet He has already provided the comfort. We just fail to look for it. **What have we missed because we neglected to see what the Scriptures had to say?**

Matthew 12:3
"But he said unto them, Have ye not read what David did, when he was an hungred, and they that were with him;"

Seven times in the New Testament Jesus asked the question, *"Have ye not read...?"* He must have desired for the people to realize the importance of reading the Scriptures, and He preserved His Word so that we could realize it too. **Whatever our situation, God's Word provides the solution; if only we would seek to find it.**

IF WE WANT THE LORD TO ORDER OUR STEPS, WE MUST STOP NEGLECTING THE WORD OF GOD.

Prepare Today.

Psalm 119:84
"How many are the days of thy servant?
when wilt thou execute judgment on them that persecute me?"

WE HAVE ONLY A SHORT TIME TO SERVE THE LORD, SO
WE MUST USE THE TIME WE HAVE BEEN GIVEN WISELY.

Job 14:1
"Man that is born of a woman is of few days and full of trouble."

Oftentimes we put off until tomorrow what we could do today.
We are not promised another day,
so we must seek to do the Lord's will while we can.

Proverbs 27:1
"Boast not thyself of to morrow;
for thou knowest not what a day may bring forth."

**The blessings God has in store for us today are found within His
Word.** We do not know what tomorrow holds, so we must not let
today slip by without seeking Him through the Scriptures.

James 4:13-14
"Go to now, ye that say, To day or to morrow we will go into such a city,
and continue there a year, and buy and sell, and get gain: Whereas ye
know not what shall be on the morrow. For what is your life? It is even
a vapour, that appeareth for a little time, and then vanisheth away."

THOUGH WE DO NOT KNOW WHAT TOMORROW HOLDS,
WE CAN CHOOSE TO LIVE FOR CHRIST AND LEARN FROM
GOD'S WORD TODAY.

Psalm 118:24
"This is the day which the Lord hath made;
we will rejoice and be glad in it."

IF WE WANT THE LORD
TO ORDER OUR STEPS,
WE MUST PREPARE TODAY
TO SERVE GOD TOMORROW.

THE PITS OF OUR LIVES.

Psalm 119:85
"The proud have digged pits for me, which are not after thy law."

Joseph found himself in a pit after his brothers left him for dead. **They meant it for evil, but God had a purpose for his life.**

The Lord brought him up out of that pit and put him in prison. When most Christians would have questioned the Lord, Joseph kept the faith. He knew God had a plan to use his life for His glory.

Genesis 50:20
"But as for you, ye thought evil against me; but God meant it unto good, to bring to pass, as it is this day, to save much people alive."

IF YOU FEEL AS IF YOU ARE IN A PIT TODAY, REST ASSURED THAT GOD HAS PLACED YOU THERE FOR A REASON.

Instead of giving in or giving up, stand still and allow the Lord to deliver you in His time and in His way.

Psalm 40:1-2
"I waited patiently for the LORD; and he inclined unto me, and heard my cry. He brought me up also out of an horrible pit, out of the miry clay, and set my feet upon a rock, and established my goings."

ALLOW THE LORD TO USE THIS TIME FOR YOUR GOOD AND HIS GLORY.
We must trust Him to deliver us from the pits of our lives.

Psalm 40:3-4
"And he hath put a new song in my mouth, even praise unto our God: many shall see it, and fear, and shall trust in the LORD. Blessed is that man that maketh the LORD his trust, and respecteth not the proud, nor such as turn aside to lies."

IF WE WANT THE LORD TO ORDER OUR STEPS, WE MUST ALLOW HIM TO USE THE PITS OF OUR LIVES FOR HIS GLORY.

His Faithful Word.

Psalm 119:86
*"All thy commandments are faithful:
they persecute me wrongfully; help thou me."*

The Word of God is Faithful,
because He is Faithful.

1 Corinthians 1:9
*"God is faithful, by whom ye were called
unto the fellowship of his Son Jesus Christ our Lord."*

When others speak lies against us, God's Word is faithful to right all wrongs. He longs to help and deliver us from persecution; though the more we are persecuted, the more the Word will be glorified.

2 Thessalonians 3:1-3
*"Finally, brethren, pray for us, that the word of the Lord may have free course, and be glorified, even as it is with you:
And that we may be delivered from unreasonable and wicked men:
for all men have not faith. But the Lord is faithful,
who shall stablish you, and keep you from evil."*

God will deliver us because His Word
tells us that He is Faithful to do so.

1 Corinthians 10:13
*"There hath no temptation taken you but such as is common to man:
but God is faithful, who will not suffer you to be tempted above that
ye are able; but will with the temptation also make a way to escape,
that ye may be able to bear it."*

Thank Him today for being Faithful
by being faithful to His Word.

Psalm 1:2
*"But his delight is in the law of the LORD;
and in his law doth he meditate day and night."*

If we want the Lord
to order our steps,
we must thank Him
for His Faithful Word.

CLING MORE TO THE WORD.

Psalm 119:87
*"They had almost consumed me upon earth;
but I forsook not thy precepts."*

The persecution we endure at the hands of others should only cause us to cling more to the Truth of the Word of God.

ENCOURAGEMENT IN PERSECUTION.

We can be encouraged that though we are troubled, perplexed, persecuted, and cast down we are not distressed, in despair, forsaken or destroyed. There is still breath in our lungs and reason to press on ahead in the work of the Lord.

2 Corinthians 4:8-9
*"We are troubled on every side, yet not distressed;
we are perplexed, but not in despair;
Persecuted, but not forsaken; cast down, but not destroyed;"*

THE PURPOSE FOR PERSECUTION.

When God allows something to occur in our lives, He always has a reason. We must remind ourselves that Jesus was persecuted so much they crucified Him. **When we are persecuted, we have the opportunity to be more like Him.**

2 Corinthians 4:10
*"Always bearing about in the body the dying of the Lord Jesus,
that the life also of Jesus might be made manifest in our body."*

Persecution is no excuse to forsake the Word of God.
Oftentimes when we need help,
we seek first to find it anywhere else but the Scriptures.

Psalm 44:17-18
*"All this is come upon us; yet have we not forgotten thee, neither have
we dealt falsely in thy covenant. Our heart is not turned back,
neither have our steps declined from thy way;"*

**IF WE WANT THE LORD
TO ORDER OUR STEPS,
WE MUST CLING TO THE WORD
IN TIMES OF PERSECUTION.**

HIS WORD GIVES US LIFE.

Psalm 119:88
*"Quicken me after thy lovingkindness;
so shall I keep the testimony of thy mouth."*

Persecution can make us feel like the life has been taken out of us; but we can find renewed life each day through the Word of God.

When we feel defeated, **His Word revives us.**
When we feel empty, **His Word sustains us.**
When we feel needy, **His Word provides for us.**

HIS WORD GIVES US LIFE.
John 6:63
"It is the spirit that quickeneth; the flesh profiteth nothing: the words that I speak unto you, they are spirit, and they are life."

HIS WORD GIVES US LIFE THROUGH CHRIST JESUS.
Ephesians 2:4-7
"But God, who is rich in mercy, for his great love wherewith he loved us, Even when we were dead in sins, hath quickened us together with Christ, (by grace ye are saved;) And hath raised us up together, and made us sit together in heavenly places in Christ Jesus: That in the ages to come he might shew the exceeding riches of his grace in his kindness toward us through Christ Jesus."

HE DOES THIS BECAUSE HE LOVES US.
Romans 5:1-2,5
"Therefore being justified by faith, we have peace with God through our Lord Jesus Christ: By whom also we have access by faith into this grace wherein we stand, and rejoice in hope of the glory of God... And hope maketh not ashamed; because the love of God is shed abroad in our hearts by the Holy Ghost which is given unto us."

God loves us so much He gave His Son to die for us, and He preserved His Word for us. **He wants us to know we have life through His Son, and we can renew our minds each day through His Word.**

IF WE WANT THE LORD
TO ORDER OUR STEPS,
WE MUST FIND THAT HIS WORD
GIVES US LIFE EVERY DAY.

THE SETTLED WORD OF GOD.

Psalm 119:89
"For ever, O LORD, thy word is settled in heaven."

God promised that He would preserve His Word for all generations.
Through the fires of worldly attacks, the Word will endure.

Psalm 12:6-7
"The words of the Lord are pure words: as silver tried in a furnace of earth, purified seven times. Thou shalt keep them, O Lord, thou shalt preserve them from this generation for ever."

The word *"preserved"* here refers to watching, keeping, and guarding. God has and is carefully watching, keeping, and guarding His Word from the changes and choices of man.

In a world where modern "versions" are constantly made, we must not be confused about what is or is not the Word of God. God is not the Author of confusion; therefore there must be a clear choice for His preserved Word. **No matter what may come our way, we can choose to stand upon what never changes.**

Isaiah 40:8
"The grass withereth, the flower fadeth: but the word of our God shall stand for ever."

HIS WORD IS SETTLED
BECAUSE IT CONTAINS THE GOSPEL.

The love of God is most truly shown in the giving of His Son, Jesus Christ; our faith in His death, burial, and resurrection is how and why we can have a relationship with God. We cannot have faith in Him without first hearing from His Word.

1 Peter 1:25
"But the word of the Lord endureth for ever. And this is the word which by the gospel is preached unto you."

IF WE WANT THE LORD TO ORDER OUR STEPS, WE MUST STAND FIRM ON THE SETTLED WORD OF GOD.

THE FAITHFULNESS OF OUR CREATOR.

Psalm 119:90
"Thy faithfulness is unto all generations:
thou hast established the earth, and it abideth."

God not only preserves His Word to every generation, but He also gives His Faithfulness to every age. As Faithful as He was to Adam in the Garden of Eden, He is still as Faithful to us today.
HE NEVER CHANGES.

He will never leave us nor forsake us because **He is Faithful.**
His mercy endureth forever because **He is Faithful.**
His Faithfulness enables us to have faith to believe in Him.
He gives us faith as a gift.

Ephesians 2:8
"For by grace are ye saved through faith;
and that not of yourselves: it is the gift of God:"

His Word tells us that His Gospel is shown through His creation.
Romans 1:20
"For the invisible things of him from the creation of the world are clearly seen, being understood by the things that are made, even his eternal power and Godhead; so that they are without excuse:"

When God created the world and all that we see, He spoke it into existence. His Word is so powerful that no labor was required. God spoke, and it happened. **The same power that created the world and raised Jesus Christ from the dead is available to us today.**

Ephesians 1:18-20
"The eyes of your understanding being enlightened; that ye may know what is the hope of his calling, and what the riches of the glory of his inheritance in the saints, And what is the exceeding greatness of his power to us-ward who believe, according to the working of his mighty power, Which he wrought in Christ, when he raised him from the dead, and set him at his own right hand in the heavenly places,"

IF WE WANT THE LORD TO ORDER OUR STEPS, WE MUST SUBMIT TO THE FAITHFULNESS OF OUR CREATOR.

WHEN GOD SPEAKS, THINGS HAPPEN.

Psalm 119:91
*"They continue this day according to thine ordinances:
for all are thy servants."*

GOD'S CREATION REMINDS US OF GOD'S PROMISES, WHICH WE FIND WITHIN HIS WORD.

As He spoke the earth into existence, so we see it today.

The land is the Earth and the waters the Seas.

Genesis 1:9-10

"And God said, Let the waters under the heaven be gathered together unto one place, and let the dry land appear: and it was so. And God called the dry land Earth; and the gathering together of the waters called he Seas: and God saw that it was good."

The sun, the moon, and the stars were placed in the sky for a specific purpose.

Genesis 1:14-18

"And God said, Let there be lights in the firmament of the heaven to divide the day from the night; and let them be for signs, and for seasons, and for days, and years: And let them be for lights in the firmament of the heaven to give light upon the earth: and it was so. And God made two great lights; the greater light to rule the day, and the lesser light to rule the night: he made the stars also. And God set them in the firmament of the heaven to give light upon the earth, And to rule over the day and over the night, and to divide the light from the darkness: and God saw that it was good."

There is a theme throughout the creation story.

"And God said...and God saw that it was good."

We can hold in our hands the very Words of the Creator of the Universe. We have the amazing opportunity to open the leather bound cover and allow Him to speak to us, and as we listen to what He has to say we too can proclaim, *"it was good."*

 **IF WE WANT THE LORD TO ORDER OUR STEPS, WE MUST REMEMBER THAT WHEN GOD SPEAKS, THINGS HAPPEN.**

MAKE HIS WORD OUR DELIGHT.

Psalm 119:92
*"Unless thy law had been my delights,
I should then have perished in mine affliction."*

The Bible teaches us to delight in the Lord through His Word.
As we delight in Him, the Scriptures then become our delight;
for He is the Word, and the Word is His Words.

THE WORD GIVES US COUNSEL.
Psalm 119:24
"Thy testimonies also are my delight and my counsellors."

THE WORD GIVES US LIFE.
Psalm 119:77
*"Let thy tender mercies come unto me, that I may live:
for thy law is my delight."*

THE WORD GIVES US COMFORT IN TROUBLE.
Psalm 119:143
*"Trouble and anguish have taken hold on me:
yet thy commandments are my delights."*

**The Word was given to us to teach us many things, including the
ultimate purpose of our lives after salvation...to glorify God.**

Romans 15:4-6
*"For whatsoever things were written aforetime were written for our
learning, that we through patience and comfort of the scriptures
might have hope. Now the God of patience and consolation grant
you to be likeminded one toward another according to Christ Jesus:
That ye may with one mind and one mouth glorify God, even the
Father of our Lord Jesus Christ."*

 IF WE WANT THE LORD
TO ORDER OUR STEPS,
WE MUST MAKE HIS WORD
OUR DELIGHT.

WE CANNOT FORGET THE WORD.

Psalm 119:93
"I will never forget thy precepts:
for with them thou hast quickened me."

Oh, that we would all say this about our lives!
May we seek to live in such a way that we cannot forget the Word of God because It has made us feel so alive. The Scriptures give us life because Jesus is the Life.

John 14:6
"Jesus saith unto him, I am the way, the truth, and the life:
no man cometh unto the Father, but by me."

JESUS IS NOT ONLY THE WAY, THE TRUTH, AND THE LIFE, BUT HE IS ALSO THE WORD.

John 1:1-4
"In the beginning was the Word, and the Word was with God, and the Word was God. The same was in the beginning with God. All things were made by him; and without him was not any thing made that was made. In him was life; and the life was the light of men."

WHEN WE FORGET THE WORD OF GOD, WE FORGET THE GOD OF THE WORD.
Deuteronomy 8:11
"Beware that thou forget not the LORD thy God, in not keeping his commandments, and his judgments, and his statutes, which I command thee this day:"

Forgetting God's Word leads to forgetting God's works.
Deuteronomy 8:12-16

Forgetting God's Works leads to wrong thinking.
Deuteronomy 8:17
There are progressive results when we forget the Word of God; and in order to avoid them, we must not forget the Word in the first place.

IF WE WANT THE LORD TO ORDER OUR STEPS, WE CANNOT FORGET THE WORD OF GOD.

HE WILL DELIVER US.

Psalm 119:94
"I am thine, save me; for I have sought thy precepts."

As God's children, the Word tells us He will deliver us from all our troubles. Whatever we face, we can have faith that He will deliver us because His Word tells us He will.
If God delivered Moses, David, and Paul... He will deliver us.

HE WILL DELIVER US FROM OUR ENEMIES.
2 Samuel 22:17-20
"He sent from above, he took me; he drew me out of many waters; He delivered me from my strong enemy, and from them that hated me: for they were too strong for me. They prevented me in the day of my calamity: but the LORD was my stay. He brought me forth also into a large place: he delivered me, because he delighted in me."

HE WILL DELIVER US FROM OUR DISTRESSES.
Psalm 107:2,6
"Let the redeemed of the LORD say so, whom he hath redeemed from the hand of the enemy...Then they cried unto the LORD in their trouble, and he delivered them out of their distresses."

HE WILL DELIVER US FROM OUR PERSECUTIONS.
2 Timothy 3:11-12
"Persecutions, afflictions, which came unto me at Antioch, at Iconium, at Lystra; what persecutions I endured: but out of them all the Lord delivered me. Yea, and all that will live godly in Christ Jesus shall suffer persecution."

How can we have faith that He will deliver us?
2 Timothy 3:16-17
"All scripture is given by inspiration of God, and is profitable for doctrine, for reproof, for correction, for instruction in righteousness: That the man of God may be perfect, throughly furnished unto all good works."

IF WE WANT THE LORD TO ORDER OUR STEPS, WE MUST HAVE FAITH THAT HE WILL DELIVER US.

CONSIDER HIS WORD.

Psalm 119:95
"The wicked have waited for me to destroy me:
but I will consider thy testimonies."

When enemies attack, **consider His Word.**
When distresses appear, **consider His Word.**
When persecutions arise, **consider His Word.**

WHEN WE CONSIDER HIS WORD, WE CONSIDER CHRIST.
Hebrews 12:2-3
"Looking unto Jesus the author and finisher of our faith; who for the joy that was set before him endured the cross, despising the shame, and is set down at the right hand of the throne of God.
For consider him that endured such contradiction of sinners against himself, lest ye be wearied and faint in your minds."

CONSIDER HIM IN CREATION.
Psalm 8:3-4
"When I consider thy heavens, the work of thy fingers, the moon and the stars, which thou hast ordained; What is man, that thou art mindful of him? and the son of man, that thou visitest him?"

CONSIDER HIM IN PROVISION.
1 Samuel 12:24
"Only fear the LORD, and serve him in truth with all your heart: for consider how great things he hath done for you."

CONSIDER HIM IN EXALTATION.
Deuteronomy 4:39
"Know therefore this day, and consider it in thine heart, that the LORD he is God in heaven above, and upon the earth beneath: there is none else."

Without Jesus Christ, we are nothing. We cannot do anything without Him, therefore we should consider Him in all that we do.

IF WE WANT THE LORD TO ORDER OUR STEPS, WE MUST CONSIDER HIS WORD IN EVERY ASPECT OF OUR LIVES.

THE LARGE PLACE.

Psalm 119:96
*"I have seen an end of all perfection:
but thy commandment is exceeding broad."*

There is no limit to what the Word of God can do or who It can reach, for It is *"exceeding broad"* or a large place.

FOR ALL PEOPLE.
Mark 16:15
*"And he said unto them, Go ye into all the world,
and preach the gospel to every creature."*

There is no person that God's Word cannot reach.
It is our job to bring them the Truth.

Romans 10:13-14,17
*"For whosoever shall call upon the name of the Lord shall be saved.
How then shall they call on him in whom they have not believed? and
how shall they believe in him of whom they have not heard? and how
shall they hear without a preacher?...So then faith cometh by hearing,
and hearing by the word of God."*

FOR ALL PURPOSES.
It directs. It protects. It informs. It transforms.
It comforts. It heals. It reveals.
**Whatever the circumstance, God's Word has the answer,
for He is the Answer to every problem.**

"thy commandment is exceeding broad."
The Word of God is a Large Place that He has given us to seek Him.

Psalm 118:5
*"I called upon the LORD in distress: the LORD answered me,
and set me in a large place."*

IF WE WANT THE LORD
TO ORDER OUR STEPS,
WE MUST SPEND TIME WITHIN THE
LARGE PLACE HE HAS GIVEN US.

A Love For The Scriptures.

Psalm 119:97
"O how love I thy law! it is my meditation all the day."

The more time we spend within that Large Place the more our love for the Word will grow.

Our love for the Scriptures will be evident in our daily lives.

Joshua 1:8
"This book of the law shall not depart out of thy mouth; but thou shalt meditate therein day and night, that thou mayest observe to do according to all that is written therein: for then thou shalt make thy way prosperous, and then thou shalt have good success."

A love for the Scriptures brings worship from our hearts.

Psalm 119:48
"My hands also will I lift up unto thy commandments, which I have loved; and I will meditate in thy statutes."

A love for the Scriptures removes the vainness from our hearts.

Psalm 119:113-114
*"I hate vain thoughts: but thy law do I love.
Thou art my hiding place and my shield: I hope in thy word."*

A love for the Scriptures enables us to share the Word from our hearts.

Deuteronomy 6:6-7
"And these words, which I command thee this day, shall be in thine heart: And thou shalt teach them diligently unto thy children, and shalt talk of them when thou sittest in thine house, and when thou walkest by the way, and when thou liest down, and when thou risest up."

God has given us the freewill to choose whether or not others can see a love for His Word in our lives. **Each day we are either growing our love or allowing it to decrease.**

If we want the Lord to order our steps, we must have a love for the Scriptures.

WISDOM FROM THE WORD.

Psalm 119:98
*"Thou through thy commandments hast made me wiser
than mine enemies: for they are ever with me."*

After Solomon had offered a thousand burnt offerings unto the Lord, God appeared unto him that night and told him to ask what God should give him. He could have asked for riches, wealth, honor, and more; yet he chose to ask for wisdom and knowledge.

**Do we have the faith to ask for wisdom
to do what God has given us to do for Him?**

James 1:5
"If any of you lack wisdom, let him ask of God, that giveth to all men liberally, and upbraideth not; and it shall be given him."

WHEN WE ASK GOD FOR WISDOM, HE ALLOWS IT TO BE FOUND WITHIN HIS WORD.

Proverbs 2:6-7
"For the Lord giveth wisdom: out of his mouth cometh knowledge and understanding. He layeth up sound wisdom for the righteous: he is a buckler to them that walk uprightly."

IT IS THROUGH THE WORD OF GOD THAT WE RECEIVE WISDOM FROM GOD.

There is no end to the wisdom He has made available to us.
The Truths of His Word are waiting for us to seek and find them.

Colossians 2:2-3
"That their hearts might be comforted, being knit together in love, and unto all riches of the full assurance of understanding, to the acknowledgement of the mystery of God, and of the Father, and of Christ; In whom are hid all the treasures of wisdom and knowledge."

Treasures of Wisdom are waiting for us within His Word.
We must only take the time to find them.

IF WE WANT THE LORD TO ORDER OUR STEPS, WE MUST SEEK WISDOM FROM THE WORD.

UNDERSTANDING THE WORD.

Psalm 119:99
*"I have more understanding than all my teachers:
for thy testimonies are my meditation."*

God had made Solomon the King of Israel just before his father, David, died. He had earnestly heeded the words of his father and remembered them that night that he asked God for wisdom.

1 Chronicles 22:11-12
*"Now, my son, the LORD be with thee; and prosper thou,
and build the house of the LORD thy God, as he hath said of thee.
Only the LORD give thee wisdom and understanding,
and give thee charge concerning Israel,
that thou mayest keep the law of the LORD thy God."*

Solomon knew that only the Lord could give him the wisdom and understanding he needed to judge God's people as king. **His father had taught him this Truth, and he understood his need for God's help in order to accomplish God's will for his life.**

Proverbs 4:1-7
"Hear, ye children, the instruction of a father, and attend to know understanding. For I give you good doctrine, forsake ye not my law. For I was my father's son, tender and only beloved in the sight of my mother. He taught me also, and said unto me, Let thine heart retain my words: keep my commandments, and live. Get wisdom, get understanding: forget it not; neither decline from the words of my mouth. Forsake her not, and she shall preserve thee: love her, and she shall keep thee. Wisdom is the principal thing; therefore get wisdom: and with all thy getting get understanding."

**AS WE RECEIVE WISDOM FROM THE WORD,
OUR UNDERSTANDING INCREASES.**

Ask the Lord to help you find wisdom and understanding within His Word today that can be applied to your daily walk with Him.

IF WE WANT THE LORD
TO ORDER OUR STEPS,
WE MUST SEEK UNDERSTANDING
FROM THE WORD OF GOD.

WISER THROUGH HIS WORD.

Psalm 119:100
"I understand more than the ancients, because I keep thy precepts."

Those who obey the Word of God, become wiser than their elders who forsake the Scriptures. Biblical wisdom allows us to become wiser than our years if we begin with a fear of Him.

Psalm 111:10
"The fear of the Lord is the beginning of wisdom:
a good understanding have all they that do his commandments:
his praise endureth for ever."

THE MORE WE FEAR THE LORD, THE WISER WE BECOME.
The more we know Him, the more we will understand.

Ephesians 1:17
"That the God of our Lord Jesus Christ, the Father of glory, may give unto you the spirit of wisdom and revelation in the knowledge of him:"

As our understanding and knowledge of Him grows,
He begins to show us what He has called us to do for Him.

Ephesians 1:18
"The eyes of your understanding being enlightened; that ye may know what is the hope of his calling, and what the riches of the glory of his inheritance in the saints,"

As we have the desire and understanding to do His will, He reveals His great power in our lives. The same power that raised Jesus Christ from the dead is the same power available to us today.

Ephesians 1:19-20
"And what is the exceeding greatness of his power to us-ward who believe, according to the working of his mighty power, Which he wrought in Christ, when he raised him from the dead, and set him at his own right hand in the heavenly places,"

IF WE WANT THE LORD
TO ORDER OUR STEPS,
WE MUST SEEK TO BECOME WISER
THROUGH HIS WORD.

AVOID EVERY EVIL WAY.

Psalm 119:101
*"I have refrained my feet from every evil way,
that I might keep thy word."*

"Oh, be careful little feet where you go."
This is a simple children's Sunday School song,
yet it entails so much Biblical wisdom.

WE MUST BE CAREFUL WHERE
WE ALLOW OUR FEET TO TAKE US.

The understanding we receive through the Word of God helps us to be able to recognize *"every evil way"* as we approach it; then, the wisdom from the Word allows us to avoid it, because we fear Him.

Job 28:28
*"And unto man he said, Behold, the fear of the Lord, that is wisdom;
and to depart from evil is understanding."*

Biblical wisdom and understanding develops discernment of that which is right and almost right. Incomplete obedience is disobedience, and we must obey the Word of God in order to please Him. We can protect ourselves from the evil way by guarding our hearts and lives with God's Word.

Proverbs 4:14-15
"Enter not into the path of the wicked, and go not in the way of evil men. Avoid it, pass not by it, turn from it, and pass away."

**Our feet will avoid every evil way as we keep our ears,
eyes, and hearts in the Word of God.**

Proverbs 4:20-21
*"My son, attend to my words; incline thine ear unto my sayings.
Let them not depart from thine eyes;
keep them in the midst of thine heart."*

**IF WE WANT THE LORD
TO ORDER OUR STEPS,
WE MUST AVOID EVERY EVIL WAY.**

Consistently In The Word.

Psalm 119:102
"I have not departed from thy judgments: for thou hast taught me."

The more we refuse to depart from the Word of God, the more we will remember what He has taught us through His Word. The Lord spoke of His consistency when He reassured Joshua after the death of Moses, and He reminds us of some Truths we can receive when we are consistently in the Word.

His Word tells us
He will never fail nor forsake us.
Joshua 1:5
"There shall not any man be able to stand before thee all the days of thy life: as I was with Moses, so I will be with thee: I will not fail thee, nor forsake thee."

His Word gives us strength and courage.
Joshua 1:7
"Only be thou strong and very courageous, that thou mayest observe to do according to all the law, which Moses my servant commanded thee: turn not from it to the right hand or to the left, that thou mayest prosper whithersoever thou goest."

His Word removes our fear.
Joshua 1:9
"Have not I commanded thee? Be strong and of a good courage; be not afraid, neither be thou dismayed: for the LORD thy God is with thee whithersoever thou goest."

**As we are consistently in the Word,
He will consistently teach us to live more like Him.**

Proverbs 4:4-5
"He taught me also, and said unto me, Let thine heart retain my words: keep my commandments, and live. Get wisdom, get understanding: forget it not; neither decline from the words of my mouth."

If we want the Lord
to order our steps,
we must consistently
be in the Word.

TASTE THE SWEETNESS.

Psalm 119:103
"How sweet are thy words unto my taste!
yea, sweeter than honey to my mouth!"

THE SWEETNESS OF THE WORD
BRINGS JOY AND PRAISE TO OUR HEARTS.

Jeremiah 15:16
"Thy words were found, and I did eat them; and thy word was unto
me the joy and rejoicing of mine heart: for I am called by thy name,
O LORD God of hosts."

Our hearts can only rejoice as we are enlightened
through the Truth of the Word of God.

Psalm 19:8-10
"The statutes of the LORD are right, rejoicing the heart:
the commandment of the LORD is pure, enlightening the eyes.
The fear of the LORD is clean, enduring for ever:
the judgments of the Lord are true and righteous altogether.
More to be desired are they than gold, yea, than much fine gold:
sweeter also than honey and the honeycomb."

IF WE ARE TO GET EVEN A TASTE
OF HOW GOOD GOD IS, WE MUST TRUST IN HIS WORD.

Psalm 34:8
"O taste and see that the Lord is good:
blessed is the man that trusteth in him."

What a reward the sweetness of the Word of God
is to our souls when we take the time to taste It.

Proverbs 24:13-14
"My son, eat thou honey, because it is good; and the honeycomb,
which is sweet to thy taste: So shall the knowledge of wisdom be unto
thy soul: when thou hast found it, then there shall be a reward, and
thy expectation shall not be cut off."

IF WE WANT THE LORD
TO ORDER OUR STEPS,
WE MUST TASTE THE SWEETNESS
OF THE WORD OF GOD.

Every False Way.

Psalm 119:104
*"Through thy precepts I get understanding:
therefore I hate every false way."*

Through the Scriptures, the Lord gives us understanding of His will for our lives to have a relationship with Him. While Jesus Christ stood upon a mountain as He preached to the multitudes, **HE NOT ONLY TAUGHT OF WHAT WAY THEY SHOULD GO, BUT ALSO WHICH WAY THEY SHOULD AVOID.**

Matthew 7:13-14
"Enter ye in at the strait gate: for wide is the gate, and broad is the way, that leadeth to destruction, and many there be which go in thereat: Because strait is the gate, and narrow is the way, which leadeth unto life, and few there be that find it."

If there are few that find the narrow way, many may profess to be Christians, yet their life tells a different story.
Christ tells us there are many and to beware of them.

Matthew 7:15
"Beware of false prophets, which come to you in sheep's clothing, but inwardly they are ravening wolves."

There are many today that have a form of godliness but deny His power. They appear to be godly followers of Christ, yet inside they are simply without Him. God gives us specific instructions on how to react when we come across them.

2 Timothy 3:5
"Having a form of godliness, but denying the power thereof: from such turn away."

We must make the choice to respond based on Biblical principles. All throughout the Word of God we are admonished to choose the right way while avoiding the wrong. Love the sinner, while hating the sin. Having compassion, while taking a stand.

**IF WE WANT THE LORD
TO ORDER OUR STEPS,
WE MUST HATE EVERY FALSE WAY.**

A Lamp & A Light.

Psalm 119:105
"Thy word is a lamp unto my feet, and a light unto my path."

**It is the Light of the Word of God that allows us
to discern the difference of every false way.**

This verse, like so many others, is often quoted, yet rarely lived. God has given us His Word to be both a Lamp and a Light as we walk with Him, yet so often we keep the Light in while our Bible is closed.

A Lamp Unto Our Feet.

A Lamp provides just enough brightness to allow us to take the next step. We can have present direction, because His Word is a Lamp unto our feet. God wants us to have the faith to trust Him each step of the way. He doesn't show us the big picture of His will all at once, but through the Lamp, we can develop faith that He will guide us through every step ahead.

A Light Unto Our Path.

His Word shines Light ahead, providing direction as to which path to take, and also allowing us to see that we are heading down the wrong one. The correction that the Word of God brings is seen through the Light. Praise God for those times in our lives that we have been redirected through the Scripture!

**When we don't know which way to turn,
the Word of God lights the way!**

Psalm 119:130
*"The entrance of thy words giveth light;
it giveth understanding unto the simple."*

The Word of God provides direction for both today and tomorrow.
He instructs us through His Word in each phase and journey of life, if only we would take the time to read and apply His Truth to our life.

**If we want the Lord
to order our steps,
we must allow
the Lamp and Light
to show us the way.**

WE CANNOT GO BACK.

Psalm 119:106
*"I have sworn, and I will perform it,
that I will keep thy righteous judgments."*

The Psalmist had promised that He would keep the commandments of God. He wanted to keep his word that he would obey God's Word.

How many times have we promised to obey the Word?
How many times have we said we would do something for the Lord?
Our promises to Him must mean something to us.

MAKING A PROMISE TO THE LORD IS A VERY SERIOUS THING.
If we do not intend to fulfill our vow to the Lord,
we should not make it in the first place.

Ecclesiastes 5:4-5
"When thou vowest a vow unto God, defer not to pay it; for he hath no pleasure in fools: pay that which thou hast vowed. Better is it that thou shouldest not vow, than that thou shouldest vow and not pay."

When we surrender to do something for the Lord, we cannot go back on our promise to Him, for He will not go back on what He has promised us. The Apostle Paul knew that God keeps His promises; and sometimes, He uses us to fulfill them.

Titus 1:1-3
"Paul, a servant of God, and an apostle of Jesus Christ, according to the faith of God's elect, and the acknowledging of the truth which is after godliness; In hope of eternal life, which God, that cannot lie, promised before the world began; But hath in due times manifested his word through preaching, which is committed unto me according to the commandment of God our Saviour;"

God chooses to commit to us the responsibility and privilege
to proclaim His Gospel to those around us.
Will we commit to do our part, so that all may know Him?

IF WE WANT THE LORD TO ORDER OUR STEPS, WE CANNOT GO BACK ON OUR PROMISE TO HIM.

Our Perspective Of Affliction.

Psalm 119:107
*"I am afflicted very much: quicken me, O LORD,
according unto thy word."*

Any amount seems like *"very much"*
when we are going through affliction.

2 Corinthians 4:17-18
*"For our light affliction, which is but for a moment, worketh for us a
far more exceeding and eternal weight of glory; While we look not at
the things which are seen, but at the things which are not seen: for
the things which are seen are temporal; but the things which are not
seen are eternal."*

**WE MUST MAKE THE CHOICE THAT, REGARDLESS OF OUR
AFFLICTION, WE WILL ALLOW THE WORD OF GOD TO
MAKE A DIFFERENCE IN OUR LIVES.**

Psalm 119:71
*"It is good for me that I have been afflicted;
that I might learn thy statutes."*

Sometimes the Lord chooses not to remove our affliction.
Paul prayed persistently for his physical infirmity to be taken away.
He believed the Lord could heal him. Instead, the Lord chose to give
His sufficient grace to Paul. This allowed His strength to made perfect
through Paul's weakness.

2 Corithians 12:8-10
*"For this thing I besought the Lord thrice, that it might depart from me.
And he said unto me, My grace is sufficient for thee: for my strength is
made perfect in weakness. Most gladly therefore will I rather glory in
my infirmities, that the power of Christ may rest upon me.
Therefore I take pleasure in infirmities, in reproaches, in necessities,
in persecutions, in distresses for Christ's sake:
for when I am weak, then am I strong."*

**IF WE WANT THE LORD
TO ORDER OUR STEPS,
WE MUST CORRECT OUR
PERSPECTIVE OF AFFLICTION.**

WILLING.

Psalm 119:108
*"Accept, I beseech thee, the freewill offerings of my mouth,
O LORD, and teach me thy judgments."*

In order for us to be willing, we must first have a giving heart.
So often when we hear the word *"offerings"*, we tend to think of ushers passing a plate throughout the congregation, so that the church can pay the bills, the pastor, or help a ministry or missionary. An offering is so much more than giving money for a cause.

2 Corinthians 9:7
"Every man according as he purposeth in his heart, so let him give; not grudgingly, or of necessity: for God loveth a cheerful giver."

AN OFFERING TO THE LORD IS ONLY AN OFFERING IF IT IS DONE WITH A WILLING HEART.
Just as God will not force us to love Him, He will not force us to praise or serve Him. God wants us to praise Him voluntarily.
He is not only worthy of our praise, He wants it!

THE LORD DESIRES OUR WILLINGNESS BEFORE ANY SACRIFICE CAN BE OFFERED UNTO HIM.

Psalm 54:6
*"I will freely sacrifice unto thee:
I will praise thy name, O Lord; for it is good."*

It is our reasonable service to offer ourselves in service to the Lord.
He only desires praise from a willing heart.

Romans 12:1
"I beseech you therefore, brethren, by the mercies of God, that ye present your bodies a living sacrifice, holy, acceptable unto God, which is your reasonable service."

May we daily submit our own desires to the Lord, willing to do His will with our whole heart.

 ## IF WE WANT THE LORD TO ORDER OUR STEPS, WE MUST WILLING.

DESPITE ANY JEOPARDY.

Psalm 119:109
"My soul is continually in my hand: yet do I not forget thy law."

David knew what it was like to feel like his life was slipping through his hands. The ruddy young keeper of sheep had fought a bear, a lion, and a giant; and yet, each time the Lord allowed him to prevail against his enemy.

1 Samuel 19:5
"For he did put his life in his hand, and slew the Philistine, and the LORD wrought a great salvation for all Israel: thou sawest it, and didst rejoice: wherefore then wilt thou sin against innocent blood, to slay David without a cause?"

DESPITE ANY DANGER OR JEOPARDY WE MAY FACE, THE WORD OF GOD CAN SPEAK PEACE TO OUR SOULS.

Psalm 85:7-8
*"Shew us thy mercy, O LORD, and grant us thy salvation.
I will hear what God the LORD will speak: for he will speak peace unto his people, and to his saints: but let them not turn again to folly."*

Even though it may seem as if we carry our lives within our hands, we must not allow anything to come between us and our walk with the Lord through His Word.

Acts 20:24
"But none of these things move me, neither count I my life dear unto myself, so that I might finish my course with joy, and the ministry, which I have received of the Lord Jesus, to testify the gospel of the grace of God."

**IF WE WANT THE LORD
TO ORDER OUR STEPS,
WE MUST BE FAITHFUL DESPITE ANY
JEOPARDY WE MAY FACE.**

Look Out For Traps.

Psalm 119:110
"The wicked have laid a snare for me:
yet I erred not from thy precepts."

In the Christian life, we must be on the lookout for traps set out along the way. Our enemies may plot against us in order to distract or deter us from our purpose, but we must not allow them to succeed.

Psalm 37:12-13
"The wicked plotteth against the just, and gnasheth upon him with his teeth. The Lord shall laugh at him: for he seeth that his day is coming."

The plots and traps of the enemy have but one true goal in mind, to get us to err from the Scriptures. **Though they may try to distract or divert us, we must stand upon the power of God's Word.**

James 1:13-14
"Let no man say when he is tempted, I am tempted of God: for God cannot be tempted with evil, neither tempteth he any man: But every man is tempted, when he is drawn away of his own lust, and enticed."

Our flesh is our greatest enemy.
The lust of our flesh craves that which God hates.
Lust leads to sin, which requires a steep payment.

James 1:15-16
"Then when lust hath conceived, it bringeth forth sin: and sin, when it is finished, bringeth forth death. Do not err, my beloved brethren."

Though traps may be set against us, we must cling to the Word of God as we trust in Him.

Proverbs 29:25
"The fear of man bringeth a snare:
but whoso putteth his trust in the LORD shall be safe."

 **If we want the Lord to order our steps, we must look out for traps.**

THE HERITAGE OF THE WORD.

Psalm 119:111
*"Thy testimonies have I taken as an heritage for ever:
for they are the rejoicing of my heart."*

WE ALL HAVE A HERITAGE.
Although we cannot decide what is left for us,
we can contribute to what we leave to those who follow us.
What does our heritage consist of?
We get to choose what we leave behind.

WILL WE LEAVE A HERITAGE
OF THE WORLD OR THE WORD?
1 John 2:15-16
*"Love not the world, neither the things that are in the world. If any
man love the world, the love of the Father is not in him. For all that is in
the world, the lust of the flesh, and the lust of the eyes, and the pride
of life, is not of the Father, but is of the world."*

If we carry the heritage of the world on to the next generation,
they will be consumed with lust and pride.
**We have the opportunity to take a stand for the truth of the Word of
God and carry His Word on to our children.**

Deuteronomy 6:6-7
*"And these words, which I command thee this day, shall be in thine
heart: And thou shalt teach them diligently unto thy children, and
shalt talk of them when thou sittest in thine house,
and when thou walkest by the way, and when thou liest down,
and when thou risest up."*

**Our heritage of the Word of God
shows the importance of the Word to us.**
Whether we make His Word a priority or only consult the Scripture
after we have tried everything else, our walk for the Lord will display
our heritage. Too often we take for granted the heritage of the Word
that we hold within our hands.

 **IF WE WANT THE LORD
TO ORDER OUR STEPS,
WE MUST TAKE PART IN THE
HERITAGE OF THE WORD OF GOD.**

EVEN UNTO THE END.

Psalm 119:112
*"I have inclined mine heart to perform thy statutes alway,
even unto the end."*

WE MUST DESIRE TO FINISH WELL,
"EVEN UNTO THE END."

Acts 20:24
*"But none of these things move me,
neither count I my life dear unto myself, so that I might finish my
course with joy, and the ministry, which I have received of the Lord
Jesus, to testify the gospel of the grace of God."*

**Finishing well will not come of our own strength or ability,
but rather, through our yielding to God and His Word.**

Philippians 3:13-15
*"Brethren, I count not myself to have apprehended: but this one
thing I do, forgetting those things which are behind, and reaching
forth unto those things which are before, I press toward the mark for
the prize of the high calling of God in Christ Jesus. Let us therefore,
as many as be perfect, be thus minded: and if in any thing ye be
otherwise minded, God shall reveal even this unto you."*

**When we depend on our Saviour, we can press on ahead
because He will always be with us.**

Matthew 28:19-20
*"Go ye therefore, and teach all nations, baptizing them in the name of
the Father, and of the Son, and of the Holy Ghost: Teaching them to
observe all things whatsoever I have commanded you: and, lo, I am
with you always, even unto the end of the world. Amen."*

What a comfort to know that He is always there for us! In Christ's last
Words before He ascended to Heaven, He commissions us to spread
the Gospel through His power and not our own.

IF WE WANT THE LORD
TO ORDER OUR STEPS,
WE MUST PRESS ON,
EVEN UNTO THE END.

OUR THOUGHTS.

Psalm 119:113
"I hate vain thoughts: but thy law do I love."

THE LORD KNOWS OUR THOUGHTS, EVEN IF WE NEVER PUT THEM INTO WORDS OR ACTIONS.

Psalm 94:11
"The LORD knoweth the thoughts of man, that they are vanity."

Our thoughts may be divided between the world and the Word.
When we try to live half in the world and half in the Word,
we are unstable and unusable for God's glory.

James 1:8
"A double minded man is unstable in all his ways."

GOD KNOWS EVEN THE THOUGHTS AND INTENTS OF OUR HEARTS, AND HIS WORD DIVIDES THEM.

Hebrews 4:12
"For the word of God is quick, and powerful, and sharper than any twoedged sword, piercing even to the dividing asunder of soul and spirit, and of the joints and marrow, and is a discerner of the thoughts and intents of the heart."

The Scriptures provide us with a defense against our thoughts before they consume us and cause us to do something we will regret.

2 Corinthians 10:3-6
"For though we walk in the flesh, we do not war after the flesh: (For the weapons of our warfare are not carnal, but mighty through God to the pulling down of strong holds;) Casting down imaginations, and every high thing that exalteth itself against the knowledge of God, and bringing into captivity every thought to the obedience of Christ; And having in a readiness to revenge all disobedience, when your obedience is fulfilled."

IF WE WANT THE LORD TO ORDER OUR STEPS, WE MUST KEEP OUR THOUGHTS IN THE WORD OF GOD.

PROTECTION & DIRECTION.

Psalm 119:114
"Thou art my hiding place and my shield: I hope in thy word."

WE OFTEN FIND OURSELVES IN NEED OF BOTH PROTECTION AND DIRECTION.

We cannot truly protect or direct our lives.
We must seek and submit to what God tells us within His Word.

THE WORD OF GOD HIDES US AND GUIDES US.

Psalm 32:7-8
*"Thou art my hiding place; thou shalt preserve me from trouble;
thou shalt compass me about with songs of deliverance. Selah.
I will instruct thee and teach thee in the way which thou shalt go:
I will guide thee with mine eye."*

THE WORD OF GOD STRENGTHENS AND SHIELDS US.

Psalm 28:7
*"The LORD is my strength and my shield; my heart trusted in him,
and I am helped: therefore my heart greatly rejoiceth;
and with my song will I praise him."*

**Only when we are protected and directed by the Word
can we have hope and faith as we walk daily with Him.**

Proverbs 3:5-6
*"Trust in the LORD with all thine heart;
and lean not unto thine own understanding.
In all thy ways acknowledge him, and he shall direct thy paths."*

 **IF WE WANT THE LORD
TO ORDER OUR STEPS,
WE MUST SEEK PROTECTION
AND DIRECTION FROM THE WORD.**

Separate Ourselves.

Psalm 119:115
*"Depart from me, ye evildoers:
for I will keep the commandments of my God."*

Just like we must evaluate our thoughts
based upon the Word of God, we must also consider
the people with whom we allow ourselves to associate.

Proverbs 13:20
*"He that walketh with wise men shall be wise:
but a companion of fools shall be destroyed."*

**May we desire to be surrounded by those
that make serving the Lord a priority in their lives
and seek to live according to the Word of God.**

Psalm 119:63
*"I am a companion of all them that fear thee,
and of them that keep thy precepts."*

While choosing to surround ourselves with those that are seeking
the Lord, we must sometimes separate ourselves from those who
have other priorities. **Separation is rarely easy.**

God will bless our efforts as we separate ourselves from worldly influences unto Him.

2 Corinthians 6:17-18
*"Wherefore come out from among them, and be ye separate,
saith the Lord, and touch not the unclean thing; and I will receive you.
And will be a Father unto you, and ye shall be my sons and daughters,
saith the Lord Almighty."*

If we want the Lord to order our steps, we must be willing to separate ourselves according to His Word.

Upheld By His Word.

Psalm 119:116
*"Uphold me according unto thy word, that I may live:
and let me not be ashamed of my hope."*

It is by God's grace that we are able to stand at all.
**We are nothing and can do nothing without Him;
yet, He chooses to hold us up through His Word.**

As we hope in His Word,
we can be sure that His Word will not fail us.
1 Peter 1:23-25
*"Being born again, not of corruptible seed, but of incorruptible, by
the word of God, which liveth and abideth for ever. For all flesh is
as grass, and all the glory of man as the flower of grass. The grass
withereth, and the flower thereof falleth away: But the word of the
Lord endureth for ever. And this is the word which by the gospel is
preached unto you."*

His Word holds us up when we fall.
Psalm 37:24
*"Though he fall, he shall not be utterly cast down:
for the LORD upholdeth him with his hand."*

His Word holds us up when we are fearful.
Isaiah 41:10
*"Fear thou not; for I am with thee: be not dismayed; for I am thy God:
I will strengthen thee; yea, I will help thee; yea, I will uphold thee with
the right hand of my righteousness."*

**Whatever our circumstance,
we can rest in God's Word while standing by His grace.**

Romans 5:1-2
*"Therefore being justified by faith, we have peace with God through
our Lord Jesus Christ: By whom also we have access by faith into this
grace wherein we stand, and rejoice in hope of the glory of God."*

If we want the Lord
to order our steps,
we must live while being
upheld by His Word.

SAFE WITHIN HIS HAND.

Psalm 119:117
"Hold thou me up, and I shall be safe:
and I will have respect unto thy statutes continually."

THE MORE WE REALIZE WE ARE SAFE WITHIN THE HAND OF GOD, THE MORE WE WILL RESPECT HIS WORD.

Psalm 73:23-24
"Nevertheless I am continually with thee: thou hast holden me by my right hand. Thou shalt guide me with thy counsel, and afterward receive me to glory."

At the right hand of the Father, our Saviour sits on His throne.
Jesus Christ, the Son of God, is the Word by which God speaks to us today. He upholds us by His power. The same power He displayed when He made our sins as white as snow is the same power with which He provides and protects every day.

Hebrews 1:1-4
"God, who at sundry times and in divers manners spake in time past unto the fathers by the prophets, Hath in these last days spoken unto us by his Son, whom he hath appointed heir of all things, by whom also he made the worlds; Who being the brightness of his glory, and the express image of his person, and upholding all things by the word of his power, when he had by himself purged our sins, sat down on the right hand of the Majesty on high; Being made so much better than the angels, as he hath by inheritance obtained a more excellent name than they."

Seek Him through His Word today and every day.
1 Chronicles 16:10-12
"Glory ye in his holy name: let the heart of them rejoice that seek the LORD. Seek the LORD and his strength, seek his face continually. Remember his marvellous works that he hath done, his wonders, and the judgments of his mouth;"

**IF WE WANT THE LORD
TO ORDER OUR STEPS,
WE MUST REALIZE WE ARE
SAFE WITHIN HIS HAND.**

Weigh The Value.

Psalm 119:118
*"Thou hast trodden down all them that err from thy statutes:
for their deceit is falsehood."*

In the context of this verse, the phrase *"trodden down"*
refers to weighing the value of something.
Light things are of little importance or value, heavy things of much.

Proverbs 11:1
*"A false balance is abomination to the Lord:
but a just weight is his delight."*

The value of our relationship
and our rewards will be weighed one day.
God, as the Righteous Judge, weighs our hearts on His judicial scales
in two specific areas of our lives.

A Rejected Relationship.
Matthew 7:21-23

A Rejected Reward.
1 Corinthians 3:12-15

**May we all weigh the value of both our relationship
and our rewards based upon the Truth of the Word of God,
for one day it will be too late to do so.**

"for their deceit is falsehood"
The profession of those who live contrary to the Word of God is a
lie. **We cannot profess Christ with our lips and deny Him with our
actions.**

2 Timothy 3:5
*"Having a form of godliness, but denying the power thereof:
from such turn away."*

If we want the Lord
to order our steps,
we must weigh the value
based upon the Word of God.

REJECT THE SIN.

Psalm 119:119
*"Thou puttest away all the wicked of the earth like dross:
therefore I love thy testimonies."*

Dross is something that is regarded as worthless.
**The wicked of the earth are unprofitable to the Lord,
and therefore He rejects those who reject Him.**

Romans 3:10-12
*"As it is written, There is none righteous, no, not one:
There is none that understandeth, there is none that seeketh after
God. They are all gone out of the way, they are together become
unprofitable; there is none that doeth good, no, not one."*

**MUCH LIKE THE DROSS IN PRECIOUS METALS,
IN ORDER FOR US TO BECOME PROFITABLE,
OUR SIN MUST BE REMOVED.**

Proverbs 17:3
*"The fining pot is for silver, and the furnace for gold:
but the LORD trieth the hearts."*

**When we choose to reject the sin in our lives,
we can become a vessel that can be used for His glory.**

Proverbs 25:4
*"Take away the dross from the silver,
and there shall come forth a vessel for the finer."*

2 Timothy 2:20-21
*"But in a great house there are not only vessels of gold and of silver,
but also of wood and of earth; and some to honour, and some to
dishonour. If a man therefore purge himself from these, he shall be
a vessel unto honour, sanctified, and meet for the master's use, and
prepared unto every good work."*

**IF WE WANT THE LORD
TO ORDER OUR STEPS,
WE MUST REJECT THE SIN
IN OUR LIVES.**

THE WRATH OF GOD.

Psalm 119:120
"My flesh trembleth for fear of thee; and I am afraid of thy judgments."

The Psalmist was not afraid of his future
but rather the eternity of those that did not know the Lord.
**HE TREMBLED AT THE THOUGHT OF THE WRATH OF GOD
BEING POURED OUT ON THOSE AROUND HIM.**
Can we say the same?

John 3:36
*"He that believeth on the Son hath everlasting life:
and he that believeth not the Son shall not see life;
but the wrath of God abideth on him."*

In Romans, the Apostle Paul pours out his heart for the same reason.
**He loved the people of Israel and wanted to see them saved
because he discerned that their profession was in vain.**

Romans 10:1-2
*"Brethren, my heart's desire and prayer to God for Israel is, that they
might be saved. For I bear them record that they have a zeal of God,
but not according to knowledge."*

Paul spoke of the difference between knowing of Christ
and knowing Him personally. **The people had the knowledge
but lacked faith to confess and believe.**

We must have a burden to reach those around us that may know of
Jesus and what He did for us, but lack a personal relationship with
Him. **The wrath of God awaits those that only have religion, having
never confessed their sin and believed on Him by faith.**

Hebrews 4:2
*"For unto us was the gospel preached, as well as unto them:
but the word preached did not profit them,
not being mixed with faith in them that heard it."*

**IF WE WANT THE LORD
TO ORDER OUR STEPS,
WE MUST FEAR THE WRATH OF GOD
THAT AWAITS OTHERS.**

Oppression.

Psalm 119:121
"I have done judgment and justice: leave me not to mine oppressors."

David knew what it is like to have enemies.
He was not a stranger to hiding in caves or running for his life. He prayed unto the Lord many times that his oppressors would not triumph over him. He had experienced the Lord as his refuge.

Psalm 9:9
*"The LORD also will be a refuge for the oppressed,
a refuge in times of trouble."*

Our enemies cannot hinder us any more than our Lord allows them to.
God is in control of our survival and our deliverance.

Psalm 27:11-14
"Teach me thy way, O LORD, and lead me in a plain path, because of mine enemies. Deliver me not over unto the will of mine enemies: for false witnesses are risen up against me, and such as breathe out cruelty. I had fainted, unless I had believed to see the goodness of the LORD in the land of the living. Wait on the LORD: be of good courage, and he shall strengthen thine heart: wait, I say, on the LORD."

**Although we may desire to get even,
we must wait on the Lord to work in our situation.**

Psalm 103:6
*"The LORD executeth righteousness and judgment
for all that are oppressed."*

God can use the oppression we face for His glory.
He may use His strength in our struggle to point others to Him through our deliverance.

If we want the Lord to order our steps, we must submit to Him through oppression.

THE SURETY OF JESUS CHRIST.

Psalm 119:122
"Be surety for thy servant for good: let not the proud oppress me."

OUR SURETY.

Jesus Christ took our place and paid the debt that we owed but could never pay ourselves.

Hebrews 7:19,22
*"For the law made nothing perfect, but the bringing in of a better hope did; by the which we draw nigh unto God.
By so much was Jesus made a surety of a better testament."*

OUR SAFETY.

The Word of God tells us many times that Christ provides safety while we journey toward our heavenly home.

Psalm 27:1
*"The LORD is my light and my salvation; whom shall I fear?
the LORD is the strength of my life; of whom shall I be afraid?"*

With God on our side we have no need to fear!

Psalm 118:6
*"The LORD is on my side; I will not fear:
what can man do unto me?"*

Romans 8:31
*"What shall we then say to these things?
If God be for us, who can be against us?"*

NO MATTER WHAT TOMORROW HOLDS, WE HAVE A SURETY IN JESUS CHRIST.

Hebrews 13:6
*"So that we may boldly say, The Lord is my helper,
and I will not fear what man shall do unto me."*

 **IF WE WANT THE LORD
TO ORDER OUR STEPS,
WE MUST REST IN
THE SURETY OF JESUS CHRIST.**

WAIT IN FAITH.

Psalm 119:123
*"Mine eyes fail for thy salvation,
and for the word of thy righteousness."*

WAITING AND HOPING FOR THE DELIVERANCE OF THE LORD CAN BE A DREADFUL EXPERIENCE.

Psalm 27:13-14
*"I had fainted, unless I had believed to see the goodness of the LORD
in the land of the living. Wait on the LORD: be of good courage,
and he shall strengthen thine heart: wait, I say, on the LORD."*

His timing is not our timing.

Many times, the Lord does not answer when we want Him to. Think of how Mary and Martha must have felt in the days after Lazarus died… but the Lord had a plan. While we wait, let us not be weary.

Galatians 6:9
*"And let us not be weary in well doing:
for in due season we shall reap, if we faint not."*

WHEN WE CANNOT SEE WHAT LIES AHEAD, WE CAN WAIT IN FAITH.

His thoughts are not our thoughts.

Though we may think that we know what is best for us, God's plan is always best. The thoughts and ways of God are much higher than ours, so why would we want to argue with Him?

Isaiah 55:8-9
*"For my thoughts are not your thoughts,
neither are your ways my ways, saith the LORD. For as the heavens are
higher than the earth, so are my ways higher than your ways, and my
thoughts than your thoughts."*

Even when we don't understand, we can wait in faith.

He is always working things for our good and His glory.

IF WE WANT THE LORD TO ORDER OUR STEPS, WE MUST WAIT IN FAITH.

MERCIFUL LESSONS.

Psalm 119:124
*"Deal with thy servant according unto thy mercy,
and teach me thy statutes."*

THE WORD OF GOD NEVER CHANGES.
The more we are in the Word, the less the waiting will discourage us. When we are discouraged, His Word can encourage us through God's mercy.

Psalm 119:76-77
"Let, I pray thee, thy merciful kindness be for my comfort, according to thy word unto thy servant. Let thy tender mercies come unto me, that I may live: for thy law is my delight."

GOD'S MERCY ENDURETH FOREVER.
Psalm 136:23-24
*"Who remembered us in our low estate:
for his mercy endureth for ever: And hath redeemed us
from our enemies: for his mercy endureth for ever."*

GOD'S WORD ENDURETH FOREVER.
1 Peter 1:24-25
*"For all flesh is as grass, and all the glory of man as the flower of grass.
The grass withereth, and the flower thereof falleth away:
But the word of the Lord endureth for ever. And this is the word which
by the gospel is preached unto you."*

There will never be a time where God's mercy and Word are not available. It is by His mercy and through His Word that we can learn some lessons that enable us to be better servants for His glory. **He is willing to teach us, if only we are willing to learn.**

Psalm 119:64
"The earth, O LORD, is full of thy mercy: teach me thy statutes."

IF WE WANT THE LORD
TO ORDER OUR STEPS,
WE MUST ALLOW HIM TO TEACH US
MERCIFUL LESSONS FROM HIS WORD.

HE WANTS US TO KNOW.

Psalm 119:125
*"I am thy servant; give me understanding
that I may know thy testimonies."*

This is the attitude that we should have each day that we live.
**We can be confident of who we are in Christ
while asking God to give us wisdom through His Word.**

Philippians 3:8-11
*"Yea doubtless, and I count all things but loss for the excellency of
the knowledge of Christ Jesus my Lord: for whom I have suffered
the loss of all things, and do count them but dung, that I may win
Christ, And be found in him, not having mine own righteousness,
which is of the law, but that which is through the faith of Christ, the
righteousness which is of God by faith: That I may know him, and the
power of his resurrection, and the fellowship of his sufferings, being
made conformable unto his death; If by any means I might attain unto
the resurrection of the dead."*

GOD WANTS US TO KNOW HIM.
Jeremiah 9:24
*"But let him that glorieth glory in this, that he understandeth and
knoweth me, that I am the LORD which exercise lovingkindness,
judgment, and righteousness, in the earth:
for in these things I delight, saith the LORD."*

THE ONLY WAY WE CAN KNOW HIM
IS THROUGH HIS WORD.

John 5:39
*"Search the scriptures; for in them ye think ye have eternal life:
and they are they which testify of me."*

IF WE WANT THE LORD
TO ORDER OUR STEPS,
WE MUST REMEMBER THAT
HE WANTS US TO KNOW HIM.

IT IS TIME.

Psalm 119:126
"It is time for thee, LORD, to work: for they have made void thy law."

Begging God to work in our lives will only work if we are also doing our part in our walk with Him. Every day that we wake up, with the breath of life God has given us, is another opportunity to seek and know Him more.

Hosea 10:12
"Sow to yourselves in righteousness, reap in mercy;
break up your fallow ground: for it is time to seek the LORD,
till he come and rain righteousness upon you."

We will give an account for what we do with the time God has given us, so we must use every opportunity for His glory.

Romans 13:11-12
"And that, knowing the time, that now it is high time to awake out of sleep: for now is our salvation nearer than when we believed. The night is far spent, the day is at hand: let us therefore cast off the works of darkness, and let us put on the armour of light."

What are we doing with the time He has given us?

IT IS TIME FOR US TO SEEK HIM.
Revelation 1:3
"Blessed is he that readeth, and they that hear the words
of this prophecy, and keep those things which are written therein:
for the time is at hand."

OUR TIME IS RUNNING SHORT.
Isaiah 55:6
"Seek ye the LORD while he may be found,
call ye upon him while he is near:"

 **IF WE WANT THE LORD
TO ORDER OUR STEPS,
WE MUST REALIZE IT IS TIME
FOR US TO SEEK HIM.**

EXPRESS OUR LOVE.

Psalm 119:127
*"Therefore I love thy commandments above gold;
yea, above fine gold."*

Often in this chapter we find a love for God's Word expressed.

OUR DEVOTION TO THE WORD IS DIRECTLY PROPORTIONAL TO OUR LOVE FOR HIM.

Psalm 119:97
"O how love I thy law! It is my meditation all the day."

"Therefore…"
THOUGH OTHERS HAVE MADE VOID THE WORD OF GOD, WE CAN CHOOSE TO EXPRESS OUR LOVE FOR THE SCRIPTURES.

Psalm 119:159
*"Consider how I love thy precepts: quicken me, O LORD,
according to thy lovingkindness."*

OUR DESIRE TO LOVE THE WORD OF GOD DIRECTLY DEPENDS UPON OUR PERSPECTIVE OF THE WORD.

Psalm 19:9-10
*"The fear of the LORD is clean, enduring for ever: the judgments of
the LORD are true and righteous altogether. More to be desired are
they than gold, yea, than much fine gold: sweeter also than honey
and the honeycomb."*

 IF WE WANT THE LORD
TO ORDER OUR STEPS,
WE MUST EXPRESS OUR LOVE
FOR THE WORD OF GOD.

THE TRUTH OF THE TRUTH.

Psalm 119:128
"Therefore I esteem all thy precepts concerning all things to be right; and I hate every false way."

Do we live as if we believe that the Truth is the Truth?
2 Samuel 7:28
"And now, O Lord GOD, thou art that God, and thy words be true, and thou hast promised this goodness unto thy servant:"

THE TRUTH OF THE WORD OF GOD BRINGS REJOICING.
Psalm 19:7-8
"The law of the LORD is perfect, converting the soul: the testimony of the LORD is sure, making wise the simple. The statutes of the LORD are right, rejoicing the heart: the commandment of the LORD is pure, enlightening the eyes."

WE REJOICE OVER THAT WHICH WE LOVE.
"Therefore…"
Our love for the Word is shown in our belief in the Truth of the Word of God. It should cause us to *"hate every false way".*

MAY WE LOVE THE WORD OF GOD SO MUCH THAT WE CHOOSE TO FLEE FROM AND AVOID ANYTHING THAT IS CONTRARY TO THE TRUTH.

Romans 12:9
"Let love be without dissimulation. Abhor that which is evil; cleave to that which is good."

How can we know the Truth of the Truth?
2 Timothy 2:15
"Study to shew thyself approved unto God, a workman that needeth not to be ashamed, rightly dividing the word of truth."

 IF WE WANT THE LORD
TO ORDER OUR STEPS,
WE MUST BELIEVE IN
THE TRUTH OF THE TRUTH.

WONDERFUL.

Psalm 119:129
"Thy testimonies are wonderful: therefore doth my soul keep them."

The Word of God is full of wonderful things because of the God of the Word. From the creation account to the end times of Revelation and every thing in between, He's Wonderful.

THE WONDERFUL WORD.
John 1:1-4
"In the beginning was the Word, and the Word was with God, and the Word was God. The same was in the beginning with God. All things were made by him; and without him was not any thing made that was made. In him was life; and the life was the light of men."

THE WONDERFUL WORD OF GOD.
Psalm 119:18
*"Open thou mine eyes,
that I may behold wondrous things out of thy law."*

THE WONDERFUL WORKS OF GOD.
Psalm 40:5
"Many, O LORD my God, are thy wonderful works which thou hast done, and thy thoughts which are to us-ward: they cannot be reckoned up in order unto thee: if I would declare and speak of them, they are more than can be numbered."

All throughout the Scriptures we find the Wonder of God, His Word, and His works.

Psalm 96:3-4
*"Declare his glory among the heathen,
his wonders among all people. For the LORD is great,
and greatly to be praised:
he is to be feared above all gods."*

IF WE WANT THE LORD
TO ORDER OUR STEPS,
WE MUST DECLARE HOW
WONDERFUL HE IS.

THE LIGHT OF THE WORD.

Psalm 119:130
*"The entrance of thy words giveth light;
it giveth understanding unto the simple."*

GOD SPOKE THE LIGHT THAT WE SEE INTO EXISTENCE, BECAUSE HE IS THE LIGHT.

Genesis 1:3-4
*"And God said, Let there be light: and there was light.
And God saw the light, that it was good:
and God divided the light from the darkness."*

THE WORD OF GOD SHINES LIGHT UPON THE DARKNESS OF HEARTS IN NEED OF SALVATION.

John 12:46
*"I am come a light into the world,
that whosoever believeth on me should not abide in darkness."*

Just as God divided the light from the darkness of the world, He has separated us from the world and unto Him.

John 8:12
*"Then spake Jesus again unto them, saying,
I am the light of the world:
he that followeth me shall not walk in darkness,
but shall have the light of life."*

As we open the pages of Scriptures, the Light of Christ shines upon us through the work of the Holy Spirit. **From the moment we read or hear the Word of God, Light shines upon our hearts.**

2 Peter 1:19
"We have also a more sure word of prophecy; whereunto ye do well that ye take heed, as unto a light that shineth in a dark place, until the day dawn, and the day star arise in your hearts:"

IF WE WANT THE LORD TO ORDER OUR STEPS, WE MUST ALLOW THE LIGHT OF THE WORD TO SHINE BRIGHTLY IN US.

A THIRST FOR THE WORD.

Psalm 119:131
"I opened my mouth, and panted:
or I longed for thy commandments."

Just like when we go for a prolonged amount of time without something to drink, our soul begins to pant with thirst for the Word when we neglect to partake of His Truth.

Psalm 42:1-2
"As the hart panteth after the water brooks, so panteth my soul after thee, O God. My soul thirsteth for God, for the living God: when shall I come and appear before God?"

Psalm 38:10
"My heart panteth, my strength faileth me: as for the light of mine eyes, it also is gone from me."

As our strength begins to fail, His never runs dry.
When we seek Him, we will never be disappointed, for we shall find Him in His Word.

Psalm 63:1-2
"O God, thou art my God; early will I seek thee: my soul thirsteth for thee, my flesh longeth for thee in a dry and thirsty land, where no water is; To see thy power and thy glory, so as I have seen thee in the sanctuary."

HOW THIRSTY ARE WE TO MEET GOD WITHIN THE PAGES OF HIS WORD?

Matthew 5:6
"Blessed are they which do hunger and thirst after righteousness: for they shall be filled."

 **IF WE WANT THE LORD TO ORDER OUR STEPS, WE MUST HAVE A THIRST FOR THE WORD OF GOD.**

Renew Our Love.

Psalm 119:132
"Look thou upon me, and be merciful unto me,
as thou usest to do unto those that love thy name."

The Lord's deliverance and mercy is only a prayer away for those that love Him. **In times of discouragement and distress, we must remind ourselves what God has done for us and renew our love for Him.**

John 3:16
"For God so loved the world, that he gave his only begotten Son,
that whosoever believeth in him should not perish,
but have everlasting life."

The Reason For Our Love For Him.
1 John 4:19
"We love him, because he first loved us."

The Rejoicing Of Our Love For Him.
Psalm 5:11-12
"But let all those that put their trust in thee rejoice: let them ever shout for joy, because thou defendest them: let them also that love thy name be joyful in thee. For thou, LORD, wilt bless the righteous; with favour wilt thou compass him as with a shield."

The Results Of Our Love For Him.
Psalm 91:14-16
"Because he hath set his love upon me, therefore will I deliver him: I will set him on high, because he hath known my name. He shall call upon me, and I will answer him: I will be with him in trouble; I will deliver him, and honour him. With long life will I satisfy him, and shew him my salvation."

Our love for God, His Name, and His Word
must be shown in our daily walk with Him and for Him.
John 14:15
"If ye love me, keep my commandments."

IF WE WANT THE LORD
TO ORDER OUR STEPS,
WE MUST RENEW OUR LOVE FOR HIM.

ORDER EACH STEP.

Psalm 119:133
"Order my steps in thy word:
and let not any iniquity have dominion over me."

We are more susceptible to giving in to the temptation we face when we neglect to spend time in the Scriptures. If we have sin in our lives, it creates a barrier between God and ourselves.

Psalm 119:9
"Wherewithal shall a young man cleanse his way?
by taking heed thereto according to thy word."

GOD PROMISES TO ORDER, OR ESTABLISH, OUR STEPS AS WE DELIGHT IN HIM.

We cannot take a single step in the right way without His direction.
Psalm 37:23
"The steps of a good man are ordered by the LORD:
and he delighteth in his way."

THE LORD CAN ONLY TRULY ORDER OUR STEPS AS WE SUBMIT OURSELVES TO SEEKING GOD'S WILL THROUGH HIS WORD.

Psalm 32:8
"I will instruct thee and teach thee in the way which thou shalt go:
I will guide thee with mine eye."

As He guides us by His Word,
He exchanges our failures for His mercy and grace.
Psalm 40:2
"He brought me up also out of an horrible pit, out of the miry clay,
and set my feet upon a rock, and established my goings."

Each step that we take by faith is an opportunity to give Him glory.
Our pits can turn to palaces as we seek His direction.

IF WE WANT THE LORD TO ORDER OUR STEPS, WE MUST ALLOW HIM TO ORDER EACH STEP WE TAKE.

SEEK HIS DELIVERANCE.

Psalm 119:134
"Deliver me from the oppression of man: so will I keep thy precepts."

BEFORE WE CAN BE DELIVERED FROM THE OPPRESSION OF THOSE AROUND US, WE MUST FIRST PURGE OURSELVES FROM THE SIN WITHIN US.

Sin causes our vessel of service to be dishonorable to our Saviour.
2 Timothy 2:19-21
"Nevertheless the foundation of God standeth sure, having this seal, The Lord knoweth them that are his. And, Let every one that nameth the name of Christ depart from iniquity. But in a great house there are not only vessels of gold and of silver, but also of wood and of earth; and some to honour, and some to dishonour. If a man therefore purge himself from these, he shall be a vessel unto honour, sanctified, and meet for the master's use, and prepared unto every good work."

NO AMOUNT OF OPPRESSION IS WORTH ALLOWING OUR FELLOWSHIP WITH HIM TO BE DAMAGED.

Luke 1:74-75
*"That he would grant unto us, that we being delivered out of the hand of our enemies might serve him without fear,
In holiness and righteousness before him, all the days of our life."*

Deliverance from the oppression of others gives us opportunity to give God praise for our freedom. His Word reminds us time and time again that deliverance is available to us, if only we will seek His help by coming to Him through His Word.

Psalm 56:10-13
"In God will I praise his word: in the LORD will I praise his word. In God have I put my trust: I will not be afraid what man can do unto me. Thy vows are upon me, O God: I will render praises unto thee. For thou hast delivered my soul from death: wilt not thou deliver my feet from falling, that I may walk before God in the light of the living?"

IF WE WANT THE LORD TO ORDER OUR STEPS, WE MUST SEEK HIS DELIVERANCE IN TIMES OF OPPRESSION.

Ask Him To Shine.

Psalm 119:135
"Make thy face to shine upon thy servant; and teach me thy statutes."

The Lord is willing to shine His Light upon our lives, if only we will ask Him to do so.

Psalm 80:1,3
"Give ear, O Shepherd of Israel, thou that leadest Joseph like a flock; thou that dwellest between the cherubims, shine forth. Turn us again, O God, and cause thy face to shine; and we shall be saved."

The Apostle Paul saw the Light of the Lord on the road to Damascus about noon. It was the brightest point of the day, and His Light shined brighter than the sun in the sky, so much so that Paul could not see. **What if the glory of the Lord shined so brightly around us that others could not see anything but Him?**

Matthew 5:16
"Let your light so shine before men, that they may see your good works, and glorify your Father which is in heaven."

The day is soon coming when we too shall look upon the face of our Saviour. His face shines so brightly in our heavenly home that there is no need for light from the sun.

The Son of God shall be the Light for all eternity.
Before we see His face, we have a commission to fulfill that we cannot do on our own.

We can only shine for Him as He shines in us through His Word.

John 8:12
"Then spake Jesus again unto them, saying, I am the light of the world: he that followeth me shall not walk in darkness, but shall have the light of life."

If we want the Lord to order our steps, we must ask Him to shine within us.

Renew Our Burden.

Psalm 119:136
"Rivers of waters run down mine eyes,
because they keep not thy law."

Where are our tears for the lost?
We must cry out to the Lord for those that do not know Him.

When we weep over the souls of men as we sow the Seed of the Word of God, He promises that we shall one day reap in joy.

Psalm 126:5-6
"They that sow in tears shall reap in joy. He that goeth forth and weepeth, bearing precious seed, shall doubtless come again with rejoicing, bringing his sheaves with him."

We must weep for them
before they weep for all eternity.

Matthew 8:12
"But the children of the kingdom shall be cast out into outer darkness: there shall be weeping and gnashing of teeth."

When was the last time
you wept for someone's soul?

Our desire to see others come to know the Lord should be evident in our daily walk for Him.

Romans 10:1
"Brethren, my heart's desire and prayer to God for Israel is, that they might be saved."

If we want the Lord
to order our steps,
we must ask Him to
renew our burden for the lost.

THE RIGHTEOUSNESS OF GOD.

Psalm 119:137
"Righteous art thou, O LORD, and upright are thy judgments."

The Righteousness of God is synonymous with His Justice, His Holiness, and His Goodness.

He is Righteous...because He is Just.
He is Righteous...because He is Holy.
He is Righteous...because He is Good.

HE IS RIGHTEOUS IN ALL HIS WAYS.
Psalm 145:17
"The LORD is righteous in all his ways, and holy in all his works."

HE IS RIGHTEOUS IN ALL HIS WORKS.
Deuteronomy 32:4
*"He is the Rock, his work is perfect: for all his ways are judgment:
a God of truth and without iniquity, just and right is he."*

HE IS RIGHTEOUS IN ALL HIS WORD.
Psalm 119:160
*"Thy word is true from the beginning:
and every one of thy righteous judgments endureth for ever."*

**The Righteousness of God is imparted to us
through our faith in Jesus Christ.**

Romans 3:22-24
*"Even the righteousness of God which is by faith of Jesus Christ
unto all and upon all them that believe: for there is no difference:
For all have sinned, and come short of the glory of God;
Being justified freely by his grace through the redemption
that is in Christ Jesus:"*

**IF WE WANT THE LORD
TO ORDER OUR STEPS,
WE MUST REMEMBER
THE RIGHTEOUSNESS OF GOD.**

THE FAITHFULNESS OF GOD.

Psalm 119:138
*"Thy testimonies that thou hast commanded
are righteous and very faithful."*

**Every Truth of the Gospel of Jesus Christ is made manifest within
the pages of the Word of God because He is Faithful.**
Romans 16:25-27
*"Now to him that is of power to stablish you
according to my gospel, and the preaching of Jesus Christ,
according to the revelation of the mystery, which was kept
secret since the world began, But now is made manifest, and by the
scriptures of the prophets, according to the commandment of the
everlasting God, made known to all nations for the obedience of
faith: To God only wise, be glory through Jesus Christ for ever. Amen."*

WE ARE ABLE TO GLORIFY AND PRAISE
THE LORD JESUS CHRIST BECAUSE WE LEARN
THROUGH THE SCRIPTURES OF HIS FAITHFULNESS.

Isaiah 25:1
*"O Lord, thou art my God; I will exalt thee, I will praise thy name;
for thou hast done wonderful things; thy counsels of old
are faithfulness and truth."*

**The wonderful things He has done are pinned
throughout the pages of our Bibles,
waiting for us to learn more of Him and His faithfulness.**

In the very last chapter of Revelation, we see yet another reminder
that His Faithfulness is shown within the Word of God.

Revelation 21:5
*"And he that sat upon the throne said, Behold, I make all things new.
And he said unto me, Write: for these words are true and faithful."*

 ### IF WE WANT THE LORD
TO ORDER OUR STEPS,
WE MUST REMEMBER
THE FAITHFULNESS OF GOD.

Renew Our Zeal.

Psalm 119:139
*"My zeal hath consumed me,
because mine enemies have forgotten thy words."*

When was the last time we had such a fervor for the things of God that it consumed us to our core? Many today have become complacent and content to just be an average Christian. God does not want us to settle for average because He is able to do the impossible in us and through us, if only we are willing to yield to Him.

A Zeal Against Sin.
The worse we see others becoming,
the more we should be encouraged to do right.
May we have a zeal to stand against any wicked way.

A Zeal For The Saviour.
We are not to compare ourselves to the conduct or convictions of others but rather to the One Who lived, died, and rose again for us.
May we display a zeal to live like Jesus.

A Zeal For The Scriptures.
In order to be like our Saviour, we must have a passion to know His Word. The Scriptures reveal to us Who Jesus is. May we decide to not only know the Word, but to apply Its principles to our lives.

Our zeal must be grounded in the Truth of The Word of God.
Romans 10:1-4
"Brethren, my heart's desire and prayer to God for Israel is, that they might be saved. For I bear them record that they have a zeal of God, but not according to knowledge. For they being ignorant of God's righteousness, and going about to establish their own righteousness, have not submitted themselves unto the righteousness of God. For Christ is the end of the law for righteousness to every one that believeth."

If we want the Lord to order our steps, we must renew our zeal for the things of God.

PURE WORDS.

Psalm 119:140
"Thy word is very pure: therefore thy servant loveth it."

**In order for something to be considered pure,
it must first be tried and refined.**
It is the object's withstanding of the fire
that enables it to be referred to as pure.

THE WORD OF GOD HAS BEEN TRIED, REFINED, AND PURIFIED BY THE FIERY TRIALS THAT HAVE BEEN THROWN AGAINST IT.

Psalm 12:6
*"The words of the LORD are pure words:
as silver tried in a furnace of earth, purified seven times."*

The Scriptures withstand any persecution because God's Word endureth forever. The Word becomes our Shield against the wiles of the devil and enables us to stand and trust Him.

Proverbs 30:5
*"Every word of God is pure:
he is a shield unto them that put their trust in him."*

Our love for the Word of God is evidence of our love for the God of the Word. Prioritize the Word of God in your life today.

MAY WE ALLOW THE SCRIPTURES TO PURIFY AND CLEANSE OUR HEARTS.

Draw nigh to God through His Pure Word today.
James 4:8
*"Draw nigh to God, and he will draw nigh to you. Cleanse your hands,
ye sinners; and purify your hearts, ye double minded."*

IF WE WANT THE LORD TO ORDER OUR STEPS, WE MUST MAKE HIS PURE WORDS A PRIORITY IN OUR LIVES.

A View Of Ourselves.

Psalm 119:141
"I am small and despised: yet do not I forget thy precepts."

David was a man after God's own heart and he had a humble opinion of himself. He knew that his worth did not depend on his own abilities or riches, for he sought the Lord's help in all that he did.

Psalm 40:17
*"But I am poor and needy; yet the Lord thinketh upon me:
thou art my help and my deliverer; make no tarrying, O my God."*

God chooses to use those that seem the most unlikely in our eyes.
1 Corinthians 1:27-29
*"But God hath chosen the foolish things of the world to confound the wise; and God hath chosen the weak things of the world to confound the things which are mighty; And base things of the world, and things which are despised, hath God chosen, yea, and things which are not, to bring to nought things that are:
That no flesh should glory in his presence."*

This is because God's thoughts are not our thoughts, and His ways are higher than our ways. **We tend to look on the outside, while God looks at the heart of those who can best be used of Him.**

1 Samuel 16:7
"But the LORD said unto Samuel, Look not on his countenance, or on the height of his stature; because I have refused him: for the LORD seeth not as man seeth; for man looketh on the outward appearance, but the LORD looketh on the heart."

Our regard for the Word of God determines our worth in the sight of God.
James 1:25
"But whoso looketh into the perfect law of liberty, and continueth therein, he being not a forgetful hearer, but a doer of the work, this man shall be blessed in his deed."

If we want the Lord to order our steps, we must have a view of ourselves based upon the Word of God.

PROCLAIM THE TRUTH.

Psalm 119:142
*"Thy righteousness is an everlasting righteousness,
and thy law is the truth."*

THE WORD OF GOD IS TRUTH BECAUSE HE IS THE TRUTH.
The Righteousness of God is everlasting;
and because He is everlastingly Righteous,
His Word is also Righteous.

**Jesus not only acknowledged the Truth of God's Word,
but He prayed that we might be sanctified through the Scriptures.**
John 17:17
"Sanctify them through thy truth: thy word is truth."

Jesus was born into this world so that He could proclaim the Truth.
John 18:37
*"Pilate therefore said unto him, Art thou a king then? Jesus answered,
Thou sayest that I am a king. To this end was I born, and for this cause
came I into the world, that I should bear witness unto the truth. Every
one that is of the truth heareth my voice."*

HE WAS BORN NOT ONLY TO PROCLAIM THE TRUTH, BUT SO THAT WE CAN PROCLAIM THE TRUTH.
As His children, we have been entrusted with the Truth of the Gospel,
and it is our privilege to carry the Truth for all to hear.

**The Spirit of Truth is Who guides us through the Truth of God's
Word.** Those who struggle with understanding what the Scriptures
have to say have not allowed the Holy Spirit to show them. We can
only proclaim the Truth as the Spirit of Truth empowers us.

John 16:13
*"Howbeit when he, the Spirit of truth, is come, he will guide you into
all truth: for he shall not speak of himself; but whatsoever he shall
hear, that shall he speak: and he will shew you things to come."*

IF WE WANT THE LORD TO ORDER OUR STEPS, WE MUST PROCLAIM THE TRUTH AS THE TRUTH.

DELIGHT WITHIN THE WORD.

Psalm 119:143
*"Trouble and anguish have taken hold on me:
yet thy commandments are my delights."*

WE KNOW WE WILL FACE TROUBLE
WITHIN OUR CHRISTIAN LIVES.

2 Timothy 3:12
*"Yea, and all that will live godly in Christ Jesus
shall suffer persecution."*

The trouble and persecution we face
does not have to take away our delight in the Word of God.
Instead, our trials should make us enjoy the Scriptures even more.

Psalm 119:77
*"Let thy tender mercies come unto me, that I may live:
for thy law is my delight."*

WE CAN BE HAPPY AMIDST OUR TROUBLES
AS WE FIND DELIGHT WITHIN THE WORD.

Psalm 94:19
*"In the multitude of my thoughts within me
thy comforts delight my soul."*

**No matter what may come our way, we can rest assured that delight
is waiting for us within the pages of our Bibles.**

Psalm 1:1-3
*"Blessed is the man that walketh not in the counsel of the
ungodly, nor standeth in the way of sinners, nor sitteth in the seat of
the scornful. But his delight is in the law of the LORD; and in his law
doth he meditate day and night. And he shall be like a tree planted
by the rivers of water, that bringeth forth his fruit in his season; his leaf
also shall not wither; and whatsoever he doeth shall prosper."*

IF WE WANT THE LORD
TO ORDER OUR STEPS,
WE MUST FIND DELIGHT
WITHIN THE WORD OF GOD.

EVERLASTING TRUTH.

Psalm 119:144
"The righteousness of thy testimonies is everlasting:
give me understanding, and I shall live."

The Righteousness that is revealed within the Word of God is the
Righteousness of Jesus Christ; therefore it is everlasting.
HE IS EVERLASTING
AND IN HIM IS FOUND EVERLASTING LIFE.

John 5:24
"Verily, verily, I say unto you, He that heareth my word, and believeth
on him that sent me, hath everlasting life, and shall not come into
condemnation; but is passed from death unto life."

HE FREELY GIVES EVERLASTING LIFE
TO ALL WHO BELIEVE ON HIM.
Our faith comes from hearing the Word of God,
and our belief in Him stems from our faith.
True faith must be birthed within the Truth of the Word of God.

Psalm 119:142
"Thy righteousness is an everlasting righteousness,
and thy law is the truth."

John 20:31
"But these are written,
that ye might believe that Jesus is the Christ, the Son of God;
and that believing ye might have life through his name."

The Word of God teaches us of a well of water
that springs up within us into everlasting life.
This Water is only available through Jesus Christ.

John 4:14
"But whosoever drinketh of the water that I shall give him shall never
thirst; but the water that I shall give him shall be in him a well of water
springing up into everlasting life."

IF WE WANT THE LORD
TO ORDER OUR STEPS,
WE MUST CLING TO THE EVERLASTING
TRUTH OF THE WORD OF GOD.

SINCERELY PLEAD.

Psalm 119:145
*"I cried with my whole heart; hear me, O LORD:
I will keep thy statutes."*

OUR PRAYERS WILL ONLY GO AS FAR AS OUR HEART WILL TAKE THEM.
If we speak words without sincerely meaning them within our hearts,
our words will be in vain.

Psalm 119:10
*"With my whole heart have I sought thee:
O let me not wander from thy commandments."*

**We must seek the Lord with our whole heart,
and we only do that by seeking Him through His Word.**

Jeremiah 29:13
*"And ye shall seek me, and find me,
when ye shall search for me with all your heart."*

THE MORE EFFORT WE PUT INTO OUR PRAYER LIFE, THE MORE OF GOD'S POWER WE WILL SEE WITHIN OUR LIVES.

James 5:16
*"Confess your faults one to another,
and pray one for another, that ye may be healed.
The effectual fervent prayer of a righteous man availeth much."*

 **IF WE WANT THE LORD
TO ORDER OUR STEPS,
WE MUST SINCERELY PLEAD
TO HIM IN PRAYER.**

CRY UNTO HIM.

Psalm 119:146
"I cried unto thee; save me, and I shall keep thy testimonies."

SOMETIMES WHEN WE SINCERELY PLEAD UNTO THE LORD IT IS FOR OUR OWN DELIVERANCE.

Psalm 71:2
"Deliver me in thy righteousness, and cause me to escape: incline thine ear unto me, and save me."

It is important that we make obedience a priority, for without it our prayers will not be heard.

Psalm 66:18
"If I regard iniquity in my heart, the Lord will not hear me:"

WHEN OUR RELATIONSHIP WITH HIM IS RIGHT, HIS EARS ARE OPEN TO OUR CRY.

Psalm 34:15
"The eyes of the LORD are upon the righteous, and his ears are open unto their cry."

He was tempted in all points like as we are, yet He did not sin. He was touched with every infirmity that we could ever have, so He knows the feelings we experience. When we cry unto Him, we can therefore come boldly unto Him to obtain His mercy and find His grace.

Hebrews 4:16
"Let us therefore come boldly unto the throne of grace, that we may obtain mercy, and find grace to help in time of need."

IF WE WANT THE LORD
TO ORDER OUR STEPS,
WE MUST CRY UNTO HIM
IN OUR TIME OF NEED.

Hope In The Morning.

Psalm 119:147
*"I prevented the dawning of the morning, and cried:
I hoped in thy word."*

Sometimes our trials keep us awake to even see the sun rising in the morning. **Even through the tears, we can choose to cry unto Him.**

Psalm 5:3
*"My voice shalt thou hear in the morning, O LORD;
in the morning will I direct my prayer unto thee, and will look up."*

WE CAN FIND HOPE WITHIN THE PAGES
OF THE WORD OF GOD, FOR HE IS OUR HOPE!

We must patiently wait on Him to work within our situation.
Psalm 130:5-6
"I wait for the LORD, my soul doth wait, and in his word do I hope. My soul waiteth for the Lord more than they that watch for the morning: I say, more than they that watch for the morning."

Jesus Christ left us an example of praying before the rising of the sun. **He purposefully set Himself apart into a solitary place in order to spend time with His Heavenly Father.**

Mark 1:35
"And in the morning, rising up a great while before day, he went out, and departed into a solitary place, and there prayed."

THE WORD OF GOD REASSURES US
THAT THOUGH WE MAY CRY,
OUR WEEPING WILL SOON BE TURNED INTO JOY.

Psalm 30:5
"…weeping may endure for a night, but joy cometh in the morning."

IF WE WANT THE LORD
TO ORDER OUR STEPS,
WE MUST SEEK
HOPE IN THE MORNING.

MEDITATE DAY & NIGHT.

Psalm 119:148
*"Mine eyes prevent the night watches,
that I might meditate in thy word."*

THE MORE WE ALLOW THE WORD OF GOD
TO CONSUME OUR THOUGHTS,
THE MORE EFFECTIVELY WE CAN SPEAK ABOUT HIM.

Our thoughts produce our words,
so why not fill our thoughts with His Word?

Joshua 1:8
*"This book of the law shall not depart out of thy mouth; but thou
shalt meditate therein day and night, that thou mayest observe to do
according to all that is written therein: for then thou shalt make thy
way prosperous, and then thou shalt have good success."*

As we make an effort to meditate upon His Word more often,
we will better understand what we should pray for as we ought.

OUR SUCCESS DEPENDS
UPON OUR OBEDIENCE OF HIS WORD.

**God has given us both the day and the night
as opportunities to learn more about Him by meditating in His Word.**

Psalm 1:2
*"But his delight is in the law of the Lord;
and in his law doth he meditate day and night."*

We can meditate upon His Word while doing something else,
but we can only meditate in His Word
when we open the precious pages of the Scriptures.

James 1:25
*"But whoso looketh into the perfect law of liberty, and continueth
therein, he being not a forgetful hearer, but a doer of the work,
this man shall be blessed in his deed."*

IF WE WANT THE LORD
TO ORDER OUR STEPS,
WE MUST MEDITATE DAY AND NIGHT
IN HIS WORD.

Lift Our Voice.

Psalm 119:149
*"Hear my voice according unto thy lovingkindness:
O LORD, quicken me according to thy judgment."*

Only those who hear God's voice can have their voice heard by Him.

John 10:26-28
"But ye believe not, because ye are not of my sheep, as I said unto you. My sheep hear my voice, and I know them, and they follow me: And I give unto them eternal life; and they shall never perish, neither shall any man pluck them out of my hand."

John 18:37
"Pilate therefore said unto him, Art thou a king then? Jesus answered, Thou sayest that I am a king. To this end was I born, and for this cause came I into the world, that I should bear witness unto the truth. Every one that is of the truth heareth my voice."

**We must lift up our voice in prayer to Him,
asking for guidance according to His will and His Word.**

The more we pray, the more our love for Him grows.

Psalm 116:1
*"I love the Lord, because he hath heard my voice
and my supplications."*

The Lord hears our prayers,
not of our merit or goodness, but through His lovingkindness.
**He never changes,
so regardless of our situation, His ears are always open to our cry.**

2 Samuel 22:7
*"In my distress I called upon the Lord, and cried to my God:
and he did hear my voice out of his temple,
and my cry did enter into his ears."*

If we want the Lord to order our steps, we must lift our voice unto Him in prayer.

DRAW NIGH TO HIS WORD.

Psalm 119:150
"They draw nigh that follow after mischief: they are far from thy law."

When we choose to distance ourselves from the Word of God, we must be prepared for the consequences. Mischief may follow us, but we will definitely see changes within our walk with the Lord.

Proverbs 28:9
*"He that turneth away his ear from hearing the law,
even his prayer shall be abomination."*

Not only will our prayers not be heard,
but also we cannot have faith without the Word of God in our lives.

Romans 10:17
"So then faith cometh by hearing, and hearing by the word of God."

Without faith, it is impossible to please God.

WE CANNOT GROW OUR WALK WITH THE LORD IF WE NEGLECT TO DRAW NIGH TO GOD THROUGH HIS WORD.

James 4:8
"Draw nigh to God, and he will draw nigh to you. Cleanse your hands, ye sinners; and purify your hearts, ye double minded."

EVERY FACET OF THE CHRISTIAN LIFE MUST BE GROUNDED WITHIN THE WORD OF GOD.
We cannot grow if we neglect to spend time in the Scriptures.

1 Peter 2:2-3
"As newborn babes, desire the sincere milk of the word, that ye may grow thereby: If so be ye have tasted that the Lord is gracious."

IF WE WANT THE LORD TO ORDER OUR STEPS, WE MUST DRAW NIGH TO HIS WORD.

HE IS ALWAYS THERE.

Psalm 119:151
"Thou art near, O LORD; and all thy commandments are truth."

HE IS ALWAYS NEAR US.
In those times when it feels like He is a million miles away, He has never left our side. **What a comfort it is to know He is always there!**

Psalm 46:1
"God is our refuge and strength, a very present help in trouble."

NO PROBLEM CAN SEPARATE US FROM HIM; NO OBSTACLE CAN STOP HIM FROM COMING TO OUR SIDE.

When our enemies attack, He will fight for us.
When trouble is near, He is just a prayer away.

Psalm 145:18
"The LORD is nigh unto all them that call upon him, to all that call upon him in truth."

When we neglect to call upon Him, we are depending upon ourselves instead of relying on His strength. When our trust is in us, we are sure to fail. When there is a distance between God and His children, it is never placed there by His choice. We must continually draw near unto our Lord, placing our trust fully in Him.

Psalm 73:28
"But it is good for me to draw near to God: I have put my trust in the Lord God, that I may declare all thy works."

 **IF WE WANT THE LORD TO ORDER OUR STEPS, WE MUST REMEMBER HE IS ALWAYS THERE.**

WHEN GOD DOES SOMETHING.

Psalm 119:152
*"Concerning thy testimonies, I have known of old
that thou hast founded them for ever."*

David knew that every Word of God was True,
and he had known this since he was a child.

WHEN GOD DOES SOMETHING, IT LASTS FOREVER.
HIS WORD IS NO DIFFERENT.
Ecclesiastes 3:14
*"I know that, whatsoever God doeth, it shall be for ever:
nothing can be put to it, nor any thing taken from it:
and God doeth it, that men should fear before him."*

This is evidence of the eternal security of the believer found in the
Old Testament. When God does something, it lasts forever. Those
who have been saved at a young age must continue to follow what
they have learned.

2 Timothy 3:14-15
*"But continue thou in the things which thou hast learned and hast
been assured of, knowing of whom thou hast learned them; And that
from a child thou hast known the holy scriptures, which are able to
make thee wise unto salvation through faith which is in Christ Jesus."*

The promise that God will never leave us nor forsake us is found in
the fact that His Word will endure throughout all generations.

GOD HAS PRESERVED HIS WORD
SO THAT ALL MAY KNOW THE TRUTH.
1 Peter 1:23-25
*"Being born again, not of corruptible seed, but of incorruptible,
by the word of God, which liveth and abideth for ever. For all flesh
is as grass, and all the glory of man as the flower of grass. The grass
withereth, and the flower thereof falleth away: But the word of the
Lord endureth for ever. And this is the word which by the gospel is
preached unto you."*

**IF WE WANT THE LORD
TO ORDER OUR STEPS,
WE MUST REMEMBER, WHEN GOD
DOES SOMETHING, IT LASTS FOREVER.**

AMIDST OUR AFFLICTION.

Psalm 119:153
"Consider mine affliction, and deliver me: for I do not forget thy law."

IN THE MIDDLE OF HIS AFFLICTION,
DAVID PRAYED TO BE DELIVERED.
He remembered what he had read and learned from the Scriptures.

Psalm 119:50
"This is my comfort in my affliction: for thy word hath quickened me."

Psalm 119:71
"It is good for me that I have been afflicted;
that I might learn thy statutes."

How comforting it is that when we find ourselves facing affliction, we can ask the Lord to help us!

REMEMBERING THE WORD AMIDST OUR AFFLICTION WILL BRING DELIVERANCE.
James 5:13-17
"Is any among you afflicted? let him pray. Is any merry? let him sing psalms. Is any sick among you? let him call for the elders of the church; and let them pray over him, anointing him with oil in the name of the Lord: And the prayer of faith shall save the sick, and the Lord shall raise him up; and if he have committed sins, they shall be forgiven him. Confess your faults one to another, and pray one for another, that ye may be healed. The effectual fervent prayer of a righteous man availeth much."

God may not take the circumstance away, but His Word can deliver our souls from the pain while shifting our focus toward our Deliverer.
Psalm 34:17-19
"The righteous cry, and the LORD heareth,
and delivereth them out of all their troubles.
The LORD is nigh unto them that are of a broken heart; and saveth such as be of a contrite spirit. Many are the afflictions of the righteous: but the LORD delivereth him out of them all."

IF WE WANT THE LORD
TO ORDER OUR STEPS,
WE MUST REMEMBER HIS WORD
AMIDST OUR AFFLICTION.

PLEAD FOR THE WORD.

Psalm 119:154
"Plead my cause, and deliver me: quicken me according to thy word."

When we finally realize that no one but the Lord can help us
we find out that He is all we really need.
**Our Advocate pleads our cause
because He is the only One Who can.**

1 John 2:1-2
"My little children, these things write I unto you, that ye sin not. And if any man sin, we have an advocate with the Father, Jesus Christ the righteous: And he is the propitiation for our sins: and not for ours only, but also for the sins of the whole world."

He desires to plead the cause for not only our sins, but for everyone.
What a shame that He continues to be rejected by those who think
they do not need Him.

2 Peter 3:9
"The Lord is not slack concerning his promise, as some men count slackness; but is longsuffering to us-ward, not willing that any should perish, but that all should come to repentance."

The Psalmist then makes his own plea,
that the Word would strengthen him during his troubles.

Psalm 119:143
*"Trouble and anguish have taken hold on me:
yet thy commandments are my delights."*

**THE MORE WE CLING TO THE WORD OF GOD,
THE MORE FAITH WE WILL HAVE FOR OUR DELIVERANCE.**
We must renew our longing for the Scriptures each day.

Psalm 119:40
*"Behold, I have longed after thy precepts:
quicken me in thy righteousness."*

**IF WE WANT THE LORD
TO ORDER OUR STEPS,
WE MUST PLEAD FOR THE WORD
TO STRENGTHEN US.**

PROCLAIM THE WORD.

Psalm 119:155
"Salvation is far from the wicked: for they seek not thy statutes."

WHEN THE WICKED NEGLECT THE WORD OF GOD, THEY REJECT THE GOD OF THE WORD.
Those that do not desire to know God
do not desire to know the Scriptures.

Job 21:14
*"Therefore they say unto God, Depart from us;
for we desire not the knowledge of thy ways."*

WHILE THE WICKED REJECT GOD, HE DOES NOT REJECT THEM.
He is not willing that any should perish,
but that all should come to repentance.
**He welcomes all who come to Him with open arms;
but they must first hear the Gospel before they can believe.**

Romans 10:13-15
*"For whosoever shall call upon the name of the Lord shall be saved.
How then shall they call on him in whom they have not believed? and
how shall they believe in him of whom they have not heard?
and how shall they hear without a preacher? And how shall they
preach, except they be sent? as it is written, How beautiful are the
feet of them that preach the gospel of peace,
and bring glad tidings of good things!"*

**It is up to the righteous to proclaim the Word of God
so that the wicked may hear and believe.**

HOW WILL THEY HEAR IF WE DO NOT TELL THEM?
Romans 10:16-17
*"But they have not all obeyed the gospel. For Esaias saith, Lord,
who hath believed our report? So then faith cometh by hearing,
and hearing by the word of God."*

IF WE WANT THE LORD TO ORDER OUR STEPS, WE MUST PROCLAIM THE WORD SO THAT ALL MAY HEAR AND BELIEVE.

His Mercy & Love.

Psalm 119:156
"Great are thy tender mercies, O LORD:
quicken me according to thy judgments."

God's mercy toward us
is a result of His love for us.

Many times throughout the Scriptures His mercies are connected with His lovingkindness. The Word of God teaches us that His mercy and love provided our salvation.

Psalm 25:5-7
"Lead me in thy truth, and teach me: for thou art the God of my salvation; on thee do I wait all the day. Remember, O LORD, thy tender mercies and thy lovingkindnesses; for they have been ever of old. Remember not the sins of my youth, nor my transgressions: according to thy mercy remember thou me for thy goodness' sake, O LORD."

Psalm 40:11
"Withhold not thou thy tender mercies from me, O Lord:
let thy lovingkindness and thy truth continually preserve me."

The Ultimate Example of God's mercy was displayed in the giving of His Son for us. He is rich in mercy because of His great love for His children. Through Christ we find life and are given a place to sit at His table in our heavenly home.

Ephesians 2:4-7
"But God, who is rich in mercy, for his great love wherewith he loved us, Even when we were dead in sins, hath quickened us together with Christ, (by grace ye are saved;) And hath raised us up together, and made us sit together in heavenly places in Christ Jesus: That in the ages to come he might shew the exceeding riches of his grace in his kindness toward us through Christ Jesus."

 **If we want the Lord to order our steps, we must thank Him for His mercy and love.**

UNMOVABLE.

Psalm 119:157
"Many are my persecutors and mine enemies;
yet do I not decline from thy testimonies."

David knew what it was like to have enemies.
King Saul abused his authority over David,
and much like today, many followed his example.

Psalm 3:1-2
"LORD, how are they increased that trouble me! many are they that
rise up against me. Many there be which say of my soul, There is no
help for him in God. Selah."

Regardless of the persecution he faced, David never turned his back
to the Law of the Lord. Instead, he chose to plead to Him for help!
Psalm 3:3
"But thou, O LORD, art a shield for me;
my glory, and the lifter up of mine head."

The Lord desires to shield us from our enemies as well.
He only asks that we ask Him for help.

WE CAN CHOOSE TODAY TO NOT LET ANYTHING MOVE US
FROM OUR WALK WITH THE LORD THROUGH HIS WORD.
Acts 20:24
"But none of these things move me, neither count I my life dear unto
myself, so that I might finish my course with joy, and the ministry,
which I have received of the Lord Jesus, to testify the gospel of the
grace of God."

As we stand unmovable, we must be busy about the Lord's business.
Our labour is not in vain if we allow Him to do the work through us!

1 Corinthians 15:58
"Therefore, my beloved brethren, be ye stedfast, unmoveable,
always abounding in the work of the Lord,
forasmuch as ye know that your labour is not in vain in the Lord."

IF WE WANT THE LORD
TO ORDER OUR STEPS,
WE MUST BE UNMOVABLE IN OUR
WALK WITH HIM.

GRIEVED BY SIN.

Psalm 119:158
*"I beheld the transgressors, and was grieved;
because they kept not thy word."*

DAVID HATED THE SIN OF THOSE AROUND HIM.
He had a burden for others to know and obey the Word of God.
Psalm 119:136
*"Rivers of waters run down mine eyes,
because they keep not thy law."*

He was grieved not because of their treatment of him but rather their violation toward God. Their offense was dishonoring and disheartening to anyone striving to bring glory to Him.

WHERE ARE OUR TEARS?
We have lost our sorrow over our own sin as well as the sin of others. There are those that profess to be religious, yet walk not in the Ways of the Lord. **Actions speak louder than words or professions.**
Psalm 139:21,23-24
"Do not I hate them, O LORD, that hate thee? and am not I grieved with those that rise up against thee? Search me, O God, and know my heart: try me, and know my thoughts: And see if there be any wicked way in me, and lead me in the way everlasting."

Our sorrow is not to be judgmental, but it is rather out of concern for the souls of others. Those who live in sin without the chastening hand of the Lord upon their lives are likely living without the Saviour.
Deception by religion is prevalent in our churches today.
Head knowledge without heart knowledge is to be tragically lost.

MAY WE RENEW OUR BURDEN TO SHINE THE LIGHT OF THE GLORIOUS GOSPEL OF JESUS CHRIST.
It all starts with our view of sin.
Psalm 119:104
*"Through thy precepts I get understanding:
therefore I hate every false way."*

IF WE WANT THE LORD TO ORDER OUR STEPS, WE MUST BE GRIEVED BY SIN.

CONSIDER HIM THROUGH HIS WORD.

Psalm 119:159
"Consider how I love thy precepts:
quicken me, O LORD, according to thy lovingkindness."

During his prayer, David asked the Lord to consider
his love for God's Word. He had previously expressed his love
and devotion earlier in the chapter.

Psalm 119:97
"O how love I thy law! it is my meditation all the day."

His love for the Word was shown in his dedication
to read, study, and meditate upon the Scriptures.
When we make God's Word a priority, God will reciprocate
that passion as He reveals more of Himself to us.

AS WE CONSIDER THE WORD OF GOD,
WE MUST CONSIDER HIM THROUGH HIS WORD.
Hebrews 12:3-4
"For consider him that endured such contradiction of sinners against
himself, lest ye be wearied and faint in your minds. Ye have not yet
resisted unto blood, striving against sin."

To rightly *"consider him"*, we must refer to the previous verse.
Hebrews 12:2
"Looking unto Jesus the author and finisher of our faith; who for the
joy that was set before him endured the cross, despising the shame,
and is set down at the right hand of the throne of God."

WHERE WE SET OUR EYES OF FAITH MAKES ALL THE
DIFFERENCE IN OUR WALK AND WORK FOR HIS GLORY.

May we keep our sight upon the Author and Finisher of our faith.

IF WE WANT THE LORD
TO ORDER OUR STEPS,
WE MUST CONSIDER HIM
THROUGH HIS WORD.

FROM THE BEGINNING.

Psalm 119:160
"Thy word is true from the beginning:
and every one of thy righteous judgments endureth for ever."

FROM THE BEGINNING,
GOD'S WORD HAS BEEN TRUE.
Genesis 1:1,3
"In the beginning God created the heaven and the earth…
And God said, Let there be light: and there was light."

God created the world through His Word,
showing the importance and worth in what He says.

THE WORD WAS PRESENT WHEN GOD SPOKE
THE WORLD INTO EXISTENCE.
John 1:1-3
"In the beginning was the Word, and the Word was with God,
and the Word was God. The same was in the beginning with God.
All things were made by him; and without him was not any thing
made that was made."

When Jesus Christ was born in the flesh, His Deity never diminished.
He was *"full of grace and truth."* The Word of Truth came to earth and
dwelt among us, the Creator among His creation.
John 1:14
"And the Word was made flesh, and dwelt among us,
(and we beheld his glory, the glory as of the only begotten
of the Father,) full of grace and truth."

THE WORD OF GOD IS AS TRUE
AS THE GOD OF THE WORD.
The Scriptures are a pure revelation of Who God Is
and what He can do for His children.

Proverbs 30:5
"Every word of God is pure:
he is a shield unto them that put their trust in him."

IF WE WANT THE LORD
TO ORDER OUR STEPS,
WE MUST REMEMBER THAT THE
WORD IS TRUE FROM THE BEGINNING.

Stand In Awe.

Psalm 119:161
"Princes have persecuted me without a cause:
but my heart standeth in awe of thy word."

Instead of fearing his persecutors,
David focused on his love for the Word.

Psalm 119:37-39
"Turn away mine eyes from beholding vanity; and quicken thou me in
thy way. Stablish thy word unto thy servant, who is devoted to thy fear.
Turn away my reproach which I fear: for thy judgments are good."

When our heart stands in awe of the Word of God, we highly regard the Truth It contains.

Those that fear the Lord have a great reverence for His Word.
Hebrews 12:27-29
"And this word, Yet once more, signifieth the removing of those things
that are shaken, as of things that are made, that those things which
cannot be shaken may remain. Wherefore we receiving a kingdom
which cannot be moved, let us have grace, whereby we may serve
God acceptably with reverence and godly fear:
For our God is a consuming fire."

Stand in awe of His Word today.
Regardless of what may come our way,
we can choose to obey the Scriptures.

Psalm 4:4
"Stand in awe, and sin not:
commune with your own heart upon your bed,
and be still. Selah."

 **If we want the Lord to order our steps, we must stand in awe of His Word.**

REJOICE AT HIS WORD.

Psalm 119:162
"I rejoice at thy word, as one that findeth great spoil."

The more we reverence the Word, the more we will rejoice in the Truth. When we allow the presence and power of God's Word to have It's rightful place within our lives, we will be overcome with awe and with joy.

Jeremiah 15:16
"Thy words were found, and I did eat them; and thy word was unto me the joy and rejoicing of mine heart: for I am called by thy name, O LORD God of hosts."

WE CAN REJOICE WHILE WE READ HIS WORD.
Nehemiah 8:8
"So they read in the book in the law of God distinctly, and gave the sense, and caused them to understand the reading."

WE CAN REJOICE WHILE WE HEAR HIS WORD.
Luke 11:28
"But he said, Yea rather, blessed are they that hear the word of God, and keep it."

WE CAN REJOICE WHILE WE MEDITATE UPON HIS WORD.
Psalm 1:2
"But his delight is in the law of the LORD; and in his law doth he meditate day and night."

WE CAN REJOICE WHILE WE DELIGHT IN HIS WORD.
Psalm 119:47
"And I will delight myself in thy commandments, which I have loved."

The Word of God is an Inexhaustible Resource for rejoicing.
Psalm 40:16
"Let all those that seek thee rejoice and be glad in thee: let such as love thy salvation say continually, The LORD be magnified."

IF WE WANT THE LORD TO ORDER OUR STEPS, WE MUST REJOICE AT HIS WORD.

ALWAYS TRUE.

Psalm 119:163
"I hate and abhor lying: but thy law do I love."

The dishonesty of others should only cause our love for the Truth of God's Word to increase. When it seems as if many around us are lying, we must cling to the One who cannot lie. Paul expressed this at the beginning of his letter to Titus.

Titus 1:1-3
"Paul, a servant of God, and an apostle of Jesus Christ, according to the faith of God's elect, and the acknowledging of the truth which is after godliness; In hope of eternal life, which God, that cannot lie, promised before the world began; But hath in due times manifested his word through preaching, which is committed unto me according to the commandment of God our Saviour;"

The promises of God are written
throughout the Word of God for our encouragement.

WHEN GOD SPEAKS, HIS WORDS ARE ALWAYS TRUE.
2 Corinthians 7:1
*"Having therefore these promises, dearly beloved,
let us cleanse ourselves from all filthiness of the flesh and spirit,
perfecting holiness in the fear of God."*

Allow dishonesty to cause you to draw nearer to the Saviour.
Ask Him to cleanse any deceit from your heart and life today.

James 4:8
"Draw nigh to God, and he will draw nigh to you. Cleanse your hands, ye sinners; and purify your hearts, ye double minded."

 IF WE WANT THE LORD
TO ORDER OUR STEPS,
WE MUST REMEMBER
THAT HIS WORD IS ALWAYS TRUE.

PRAISE HIM FOR HIS WORD.

Psalm 119:164
*"Seven times a day do I praise thee
because of thy righteous judgments."*

DAVID WAS FAITHFUL TO PRAISE THE LORD BECAUSE HE BELIEVED IN THE RIGHTEOUSNESS OF HIS WORD.

Psalm 56:4
*"In God I will praise his word, in God I have put my trust;
I will not fear what flesh can do unto me."*

Psalm 56:10
"In God will I praise his word: in the LORD will I praise his word."

Our faithfulness, or lack thereof, in praising the Lord for the Word of God is displayed in daily living. When we love Him with all of our heart, it is shown through our actions and words. The purpose of our lives is to give praise to Him.

Psalm 138:1-2
"I will praise thee with my whole heart: before the gods will I sing praise unto thee. I will worship toward thy holy temple, and praise thy name for thy lovingkindness and for thy truth: for thou hast magnified thy word above all thy name."

The magnitude of the Word of God is shown in this passage. As powerful and wonderful as the Name of Jesus is, the Lord has chosen to magnify His Word even above His Name. **May we praise His Word in the Name that is above every name, the Name of Jesus!**

Ephesians 5:20
"Giving thanks always for all things unto God and the Father in the name of our Lord Jesus Christ;"

In the midst of discouragement, despair or depression,
we can still praise the Lord!
**Regardless of what goes on in our lives,
we can praise Him for His Word.**

IF WE WANT THE LORD TO ORDER OUR STEPS, WE MUST PRAISE HIM FOR HIS WORD DESPITE OUR CIRCUMSTANCES.

UNOFFENDABLE.

Psalm 119:165
*"Great peace have they which love thy law:
and nothing shall offend them."*

When we truly love the Word of God,
we are promised to have not just peace, but great peace.
This peace can only come from our Lord Jesus Christ.

HE CAN GIVE US A SATISFACTION THAT CANNOT BE FOUND WITHIN THE WORLD, BUT RATHER ONLY IN HIS WORD.

John 14:27
*"Peace I leave with you, my peace I give unto you:
not as the world giveth, give I unto you.
Let not your heart be troubled, neither let it be afraid."*

JESUS CHRIST PROMISED TO GIVE US PEACE.
The simple requirement is that we love His Word.
Our love for the Word is shown when we become unoffendable.

When we apply the Truth of God's Word, that He is working everything for our good and His glory to our lives, we find that great peace. There is no explanation that warrants the vastness of the peace of God from His Word.

Philippians 4:7
"And the peace of God, which passeth all understanding, shall keep your hearts and minds through Christ Jesus."

KEEP YOUR HEART AND MIND ON HIM TODAY.
REST IN HIS PEACE.

Isaiah 26:3
*"Thou wilt keep him in perfect peace, whose mind is stayed on thee:
because he trusteth in thee."*

**IF WE WANT THE LORD
TO ORDER OUR STEPS,
WE CAN STRIVE TO BE UNOFFENDABLE
THROUGH HIS WORD.**

FAITHFULLY WAITING.

Psalm 119:166
"LORD, I have hoped for thy salvation, and done thy commandments."

Having hope is to faithfully wait for God to move in your situation.
When we reach the point of wanting to give up, we can increase our
faith through the Word of God.

Psalm 119:81
"My soul fainteth for thy salvation: but I hope in thy word."

FAITHFULLY WAITING BRINGS PROTECTION.
Psalm 119:114
"Thou art my hiding place and my shield: I hope in thy word."

FAITHFULLY WAITING BRINGS PROVISION.
Psalm 119:116
*"Uphold me according unto thy word, that I may live:
and let me not be ashamed of my hope."*

**The Word of God provides us protection
while we wait on Him to move on our behalf.**
Trust Him today.

ALLOW HIS WORD TO COMFORT AND ENCOURAGE
YOU WHILE YOU WAIT.

Psalm 130:5-6
*"I wait for the LORD, my soul doth wait, and in his word do I hope.
My soul waiteth for the Lord
more than they that watch for the morning:
I say, more than they that watch for the morning."*

IF WE WANT THE LORD
TO ORDER OUR STEPS,
WE MUST OBEY HIS WORD WHILE
FAITHFULLY WAITING ON HIM.

EXCEEDINGLY.

Psalm 119:167
"My soul hath kept thy testimonies; and I love them exceedingly."

Our love for the Scriptures is best shown to the Saviour by our obedience to His Word. We are blessed to have the Word of God, and we must keep the Word to express our love for Him.

John 14:21
"He that hath my commandments, and keepeth them, he it is that loveth me: and he that loveth me shall be loved of my Father, and I will love him, and will manifest myself to him."

WHEN WE LOVE THE WORD, HE WILL MANIFEST HIS PRESENCE TO US.
The more time we spend searching and studying the Scriptures, the more of Him we can experience.
We can hold His Word with our hands and our hearts.

1 John 1:1-3
"That which was from the beginning, which we have heard, which we have seen with our eyes, which we have looked upon, and our hands have handled, of the Word of life; (For the life was manifested, and we have seen it, and bear witness, and shew unto you that eternal life, which was with the Father, and was manifested unto us;) That which we have seen and heard declare we unto you, that ye also may have fellowship with us: and truly our fellowship is with the Father, and with his Son Jesus Christ."

OUR FELLOWSHIP WITH GOD WILL EXCEEDINGLY GROW OUR LOVE FOR HIM AND HIS WORD.
We have no communion with Him if we do not obey the Scriptures.

1 John 1:6
"If we say that we have fellowship with him, and walk in darkness, we lie, and do not the truth:"

IF WE WANT THE LORD TO ORDER OUR STEPS, WE MUST LOVE HIS WORD EXCEEDINGLY.

OBEY HIS WAYS.

Psalm 119:168
*"I have kept thy precepts and thy testimonies:
for all my ways are before thee."*

GOD SEES EVERY STEP THAT WE TAKE
AS WE WALK BEFORE HIM.
Nothing can be hidden from the Lord
because He alone knows our hearts.

Psalm 139:1-3
*"O LORD, thou hast searched me, and known me.
Thou knowest my downsitting and mine uprising, thou understandest
my thought afar off. Thou compassest my path and my lying down,
and art acquainted with all my ways."*

Since He knows all our ways, should we not seek to obey?
The omniscience of God should motivate us to live as His Word
teaches. He knows everything about us; yet He still loves us.
He loves us so much that He sent His Son to die for our sins.

HE SEES OUR WAYS BECAUSE HE IS THE WAY.

John 14:6
*"Jesus saith unto him, I am the way, the truth, and the life:
no man cometh unto the Father, but by me."*

THE WORD OF GOD IS THE WAY OF GOD.
May we desire today to earnestly obey His Way
as we walk through His Word.

Psalm 119:101
*"I have refrained my feet from every evil way,
that I might keep thy word."*

Psalm 128:1
"Blessed is every one that feareth the LORD; that walketh in his ways."

IF WE WANT THE LORD
TO ORDER OUR STEPS,
WE MUST OBEY HIS WAYS.

EVALUATE OUR CRY.

Psalm 119:169
*"Let my cry come near before thee, O LORD:
give me understanding according to thy word."*

THE LORD HEARS OUR PRAYERS
WHEN WE CRY UNTO HIM.
When we come into His presence, He hears our voice even if we do not utter any words. He hears our hearts.

Psalm 18:6
*"In my distress I called upon the LORD, and cried unto my God:
he heard my voice out of his temple, and my cry came before him,
even into his ears."*

Psalm 61:1-2
*"Hear my cry, O God; attend unto my prayer. From the end of the
earth will I cry unto thee, when my heart is overwhelmed: lead me to
the rock that is higher than I."*

The question is what is our intent when we cry unto Him?
When we are distressed or overwhelmed, we must choose how we respond in our prayers. Complaining, pleading, and asking are forms of crying out to the Lord; but notice what was asked for in today's verse, *"…give me understanding according to thy word."*

WHEN WE CRY UNTO THE LORD,
WE MUST APPRAISE THE NATURE OF OUR PRAYER.
He hears our complaints, our pleas for deliverance, as well as our asking for understanding while enduring our affliction. Such wisdom can only found within the pages of the Word of God.

Proverbs 2:6
*"For the LORD giveth wisdom:
out of his mouth cometh knowledge and understanding."*

IF WE WANT THE LORD
TO ORDER OUR STEPS,
WE MUST EVALUATE OUR CRY UNTO
HIM BASED UPON HIS WORD.

MAKE OUR REQUESTS KNOWN.

Psalm 119:170
"Let my supplication come before thee:
deliver me according to thy word."

Similar to the previous verse,
we again find a reference to our prayer coming before the Lord.
Rather than a cry, there is a supplication made.
A PRAYER OF SUPPLICATION ALWAYS INVOLVES
A REQUEST BEING MADE UNTO GOD.

Philippians 4:6
"Be careful for nothing; but in every thing by prayer and supplication
with thanksgiving let your requests be made known unto God."

When we offer a supplication unto the Lord, our request is to be
submitted earnestly and humbly. Our humility is met with the mercy
and grace of God as we bring our need before Him, allowing Him to
work in our situation as only He can.

1 Samuel 1:10-11
"And she was in bitterness of soul, and prayed unto the LORD,
and wept sore. And she vowed a vow, and said, O LORD of hosts,
if thou wilt indeed look on the affliction of thine handmaid, and
remember me, and not forget thine handmaid, but wilt give unto
thine handmaid a man child, then I will give him unto the LORD all
the days of his life, and there shall no razor come upon his head."

Hannah prayed so fervently unto the Lord that Eli thought she was
drunk. She poured out her soul before the Lord in prayer. She
sincerely asked with humility, and the Lord gave her Samuel. Her
supplication preceded God's provision. When there appeared to be
no way, she pleaded for the Lord to intervene.

How would your prayer life compare to hers?

IF WE WANT THE LORD
TO ORDER OUR STEPS,
WE MUST MAKE OUR REQUESTS
KNOWN UNTO HIM.

SPEAK OUR PRAISE.

Psalm 119:171
"My lips shall utter praise, when thou hast taught me thy statutes."

SUPPLICATION IS OFTEN FOLLOWED BY PRAISE.

When a request we have made unto God is fulfilled,
we should worship Him for His provision and grace.
His Word tells us of His promises.

Matthew 7:7-8
"Ask, and it shall be given you; seek, and ye shall find; knock, and it shall be opened unto you: For every one that asketh receiveth; and he that seeketh findeth; and to him that knocketh it shall be opened."

Many times throughout Psalm 119,
we see an asking or reference to being taught from the Word of God.

The previous two verses, before our text today,
end with *"according to thy word."*
**When our perspective and pursuit are according to
what the Word of the Lord says, we cannot fail.**

Luke 6:45
"A good man out of the good treasure of his heart bringeth forth that which is good; and an evil man out of the evil treasure of his heart bringeth forth that which is evil: for of the abundance of the heart his mouth speaketh."

Our voice unveils the condition of our heart.
We speak what we know and believe.

THE MORE WE ARE IN THE WORD, THE MORE OUR WORDS WILL REFLECT THE WORD.

**IF WE WANT THE LORD
TO ORDER OUR STEPS,
WE MUST SPEAK OUR PRAISE
ACCORDING TO HIS WORD.**

SPEAK HIS WORD.

Psalm 119:172
"My tongue shall speak of thy word:
for all thy commandments are righteousness."

Our supplication brings forth praise to the Lord for what He has done; and then that praise leads to speaking of the Truth of God's Word.

MAY THE WORD OF THE LORD BE EVER IN OUR HEARTS SO THAT WE CAN SPEAK HIS WORD CONTINUALLY.

Psalm 138:1-2
"I will praise thee with my whole heart: before the gods will I sing praise unto thee. I will worship toward thy holy temple, and praise thy name for thy lovingkindness and for thy truth: for thou hast magnified thy word above all thy name."

The Lord magnifies His Word above all His Name, showing us the importance of reading and applying the Word of God to our lives so that we may share Him with others.

Deuteronomy 6:5-7
"And thou shalt love the LORD thy God with all thine heart, and with all thy soul, and with all thy might. And these words, which I command thee this day, shall be in thine heart: And thou shalt teach them diligently unto thy children, and shalt talk of them when thou sittest in thine house, and when thou walkest by the way, and when thou liest down, and when thou risest up."

When we love the Lord with all of our hearts,
we will not only speak often of His Word,
but also desire to teach others what we have found to be true.

IF WE WANT THE LORD TO ORDER OUR STEPS, WE MUST SPEAK HIS WORD SO THAT OTHERS MAY HEAR.

CHOOSE HIS WORD.

Psalm 119:173
"Let thine hand help me; for I have chosen thy precepts."

EACH DAY WE HAVE CHOICES
TO MAKE IN OUR WALK WITH THE LORD.

Mary and Martha, the sisters of Lazarus, show us how we must choose
even our method of service to the Lord.
Both had good intentions and the desire to serve,
but Jesus spoke of the difference between them.

Luke 10:39-42
*"And she had a sister called Mary, which also sat at Jesus' feet, and
heard his word. But Martha was cumbered about much serving,
and came to him, and said, Lord, dost thou not care that my sister
hath left me to serve alone? bid her therefore that she help me. And
Jesus answered and said unto her, Martha, Martha, thou art careful
and troubled about many things: But one thing is needful: and Mary
hath chosen that good part, which shall not be taken away from her."*

**Martha chose to serve the Lord in her own understanding,
while Mary chose to sit at His feet and hear His Word.**

Proverbs 3:5
*"Trust in the LORD with all thine heart;
and lean not unto thine own understanding."*

This popular verse is within the context of blessings that are
available when we choose to make the Word of God a priority.
Trusting in the Lord is to trust in His Word.

RATHER THAN LEANING ON OUR OWN UNDERSTANDING,
WE CAN CHOOSE TO FIND UNDERSTANDING
THROUGH HIS WORD.

**IF WE WANT THE LORD
TO ORDER OUR STEPS,
WE MUST CHOOSE HIS WORD
EACH DAY.**

TRUE DELIGHT.

Psalm 119:174
"I have longed for thy salvation, O LORD; and thy law is my delight."

Delighting in something is to find gladness or pleasure in it.
**We can receive delight from many things in this world,
but true delight only comes from the Lord.**

Psalm 37:4
*"Delight thyself also in the LORD;
and he shall give thee the desires of thine heart."*

WHEN WE DELIGHT IN HIM, OUR DESIRES BEGIN TO ALIGN WITH HIS WILL FOR OUR LIVES.
This does not mean that the Lord simply gives us what we want,
but rather we yield our own will for His.

Psalm 1:1-2
*"Blessed is the man that walketh not in the counsel of the
ungodly, nor standeth in the way of sinners, nor sitteth in the seat of
the scornful. But his delight is in the law of the LORD; and in his law
doth he meditate day and night."*

TRUE DELIGHT IS FOUND
WITHIN THE PAGES OF THE WORD OF GOD.

May we seek today to find gladness in the Scriptures.
**Our delight in the Lord is directly proportional
to our love for His Word.**

Psalm 119:47
*"And I will delight myself in thy commandments,
which I have loved."*

IF WE WANT THE LORD
TO ORDER OUR STEPS,
WE MUST FIND TRUE DELIGHT
IN HIS WORD.

OUR PURPOSE.

Psalm 119:175
*"Let my soul live, and it shall praise thee;
and let thy judgments help me."*

EVERY BREATH WE TAKE IS A GIFT FROM GOD.

Here we find the Psalmist asking for more time to live,
not for his own pleasure or purpose, but so that he may offer more
praise unto the Creator. When God breathed into Adam's nostrils the
breath of life, man became a living soul.

THE PURPOSE OF MAN HAS ALWAYS BEEN TO COMMUNE WITH AND TO WORSHIP THE LORD GOD.

Isaiah 43:7
*"Even every one that is called by my name: for I have created him for
my glory, I have formed him; yea, I have made him."*

However, because we are born into Adam's sin,
we cannot come to God on our own.
Sin separates our fellowship with Him;
but God gave His only begotten Son,
so that we may have eternal life through Him.

OUR PURPOSE IS RESTORED THROUGH THE BLOOD OF JESUS CHRIST.

Romans 3:23-24
*"For all have sinned, and come short of the glory of God;
Being justified freely by his grace through the redemption
that is in Christ Jesus:"*

**Only the redeemed can truly worship God as they yield to the Spirit
of God through the Truth found within His Word.** We either worship
God *"in spirit and in truth"* or we do not worship Him at all.

John 4:24
*"God is a Spirit: and they that worship him
must worship him in spirit and in truth."*

 **IF WE WANT THE LORD
TO ORDER OUR STEPS,
WE MUST REMEMBER OUR PURPOSE
IS TO WORSHIP HIM.**

His Word Remains.

Psalm 119:176
"I have gone astray like a lost sheep; seek thy servant;
for I do not forget thy commandments."

After praying, pleading, and praising throughout the chapter,
the Psalmist uses the last verse to summarize the ongoing theme.

"I have gone astray like a lost sheep…"
We must acknowledge our condition before God.
Our relationship cannot change, but our fellowship can fluctuate.

Psalm 23:1-2
"The LORD is my shepherd; I shall not want. He maketh me to lie
down in green pastures: he leadeth me beside the still waters."
He is our Shepherd, and we are His sheep.

"…seek thy servant…"
Acknowledging our need for assistance is only the first step.
We must then ask for the Lord's intervention.

Psalm 23:3
"He restoreth my soul: he leadeth me
in the paths of righteousness for his name's sake."
He waits until we ask, but never fails to rescue His sheep once we are
willing to be found. **He then willingly leads us in the right direction.**

"…for I do not forget thy commandments."
Even when we go astray in our walk with the Lord,
our respect and love for His Word remains within us.

Psalm 23:4
"Yea, though I walk through the valley of the shadow of death,
I will fear no evil: for thou art with me;
thy rod and thy staff they comfort me."

The Word of God brings us comfort unlike anything else can.

If we want the Lord
to order our steps,
we must remember that when
all else fails, His Word remains.

OUR STEPS BECOME ORDERED BY THE LORD WHEN WE DELIGHT IN HIS WORD.

Psalm 37:23
"The steps of a good man are ordered by the LORD: and he delighteth in his way."

ABOUT US

"Delight thyself also in the LORD;
and he shall give thee the desires of thine heart."
Psalm 37:4

From this verse comes the inspiration behind the name of this ministry. It is a reminder that if we delight ourselves in Him, He promises to give us desires according to His will for our lives.

In 2012, the desire for a design ministry began. The Lord has since opened door after door to allow that desire to become a reality..."*Commit thy way unto the LORD; trust also in him; and he shall bring it to pass."* Psalm 37:5

Delight Thyself Design Ministries began as a media ministry at Teays Valley Baptist Church of Hurricane, WV. Shortly after that, the Lord began to direct us toward reaching people with the printed Word of the Gospel. A tract ministry was born, and has since continued to grow as the Lord leads. In 2014, we began shipping tracts to missionaries across the world with little to no material with which to reach their field. **Please pray with us** that the Lord will continue to provide resources to print the tracts the missionaries are requesting.

We ship tracts free of charge to anyone willing to distribute the printed Word of the Gospel of Jesus Christ. Contact us if you would like to receive a sample pack or box to distribute.

Gospel tracts customized with a church's contact information are a great way to spread the Gospel and allow others to contact your ministry. We also design custom material for Independent Baptist Churches, which helps fund the printing and distribution of Gospel tracts which are sent across the world.

We are so thankful for those whom the Lord has provided to support this ministry on a monthly basis or through one time donations. If it were not for these people, this ministry could not exist today. We claim Philippians 4:17 for this method of support, *"Not because I desire a gift: but I desire fruit that may abound to your account."*

If you would like to receive ministry updates, follow us on social media or send us your email address to receive our newsletters.

Delight Thyself also in the Lord

A SIMPLE DAILY DEVOTIONAL

Available on Amazon & delightthyself.com

Delight Thyself

DESIGN MINISTRIES

We invite you to sign up for our online daily devotional at delightthyself.com/devotional

Each day features a verse to fit the current theme, a short devotional, and a Bible reading schedule.

THE BIBLE WAY TO HEAVEN

*"Jesus saith unto him, I am the way, the truth, and the life;
no man cometh unto the Father, but by me."*
John 14:6

We Are All Sinners.
"For all have sinned, and come short of the glory of God."
Romans 3:23

We Were Sent A Saviour.
*"But God commendeth his love toward us, in that,
while we were yet sinners, Christ died for us."*
Romans 5:8

We Were Supplied A Gift.
*"For the wages of sin is death;
but the gift of God is eternal life through Jesus Christ our Lord."*
Romans 6:23

We Can Simply Confess & Call.
*"That if thou shalt confess with thy mouth the Lord Jesus,
and shalt believe in thine heart that God
hath raised him from the dead, thou shalt be saved.
For whosoever shall call upon the name of the Lord shall be saved."*
Romans 10:9,13

It's that simple.

The Bible says... **Whosoever.**
Once you see yourself as a sinner, if you will simply *"call upon the name of the Lord"*, you can be saved from spending eternity in the Lake of Fire separated from God. You may say..."It's not for me," or "I'll never be good enough", but God said... **Whosoever.**

God is not willing that any should perish.
That includes you.

If you have trusted Christ as your Saviour,
or would like more information, please contact us.

delightthyself.com